Social Dilemmas

Social Dilemmas

SAMUEL S. KOMORITA
University of Illinois

CRAIG D. PARKS
Siena College

Brown &
Benchmark

PUBLISHERS

Madison, Wisconsin · Dubuque, Iowa

Book Team

Executive Editor *Michael Lange*
Developmental Editor *Ted Underhill*
Production Editor *Gloria G. Schiesl*
Visuals/Design Developmental Consultant *Marilyn A. Phelps*
Visuals/Design Freelance Specialist *Mary L. Christianson*
Marketing Manager *Elizabeth Haefele*
Advertising Manager *Nancy Milling*

 Brown & Benchmark

A Division of Wm. C. Brown Communications, Inc.

Executive Vice President/General Manager *Thomas E. Doran*
Vice President/Editor in Chief *Edgar J. Laube*
Vice President/Sales and Marketing *Eric Ziegler*
Director of Production *Vickie Putman Caughron*
Director of Custom and Electronic Publishing *Chris Rogers*

Wm. C. Brown Communications, Inc.

President and Chief Executive Officer *G. Franklin Lewis*
Corporate Senior Vice President and Chief Financial Officer *Robert Chesterman*
Corporate Senior Vice President and President of Manufacturing *Roger Meyer*

Brown & Benchmark's Social Psychology Series
Consulting Editor: John Harvey, University of Iowa

Cover design by Marilyn Phelps

Cover image by Claude Monet (1840–1926) *Boulevard des Capucines,*
1873–74. Oil on canvas: 31-3/4″ × 23-13/16″ (79.4 × 60.6 cm.)
The Nelson-Atkins Museum of Art, Kansas City, Missouri
(Purchase: the Kenneth A. and Helen F. Spencer Foundation Acquisition
Fund) F72–35.

Copyedited by Maureen Peifer

Copyright © 1994 by Wm. C. Brown Communications, Inc.
All rights reserved

A Times Mirror Company

Library of Congress Catalog Card Number: 93–71363

ISBN 0–697–15026–7

Printed in the United States of America by Wm. C. Brown Communications, Inc.,
2460 Kerper Boulevard, Dubuque, IA 52001

10 9 8 7 6 5 4 3

CONTENTS

6 Social Dilemmas and Interdisciplinary Issues   124

7 Summary and Conclusions   151

PREFACE

A social dilemma is that rare topic in psychology that appeals not only to psychologists, but also to researchers in many other disciplines: economists, sociologists, political scientists, and biologists all have done extensive work on the topic. Besides its broad appeal, the popularity of social dilemma research is growing rapidly. During the four-year period from 1976 to 1980, a total of 6 psychological (behavioral) studies of social dilemmas were published; from 1981 to 1985, 33 were published; and from 1986 to 1990, 51 were published.

Our purpose in writing this book is to provide a summary and integration of the psychological research, and to introduce readers to some of the work being done in other disciplines. The question that occupies most psychologists working in this area is, "How can we encourage people to be more cooperative?" This is the basic theme of our book and we shall attempt to answer this question for a variety of social dilemma situations.

Research on social dilemmas is also important because they are so pervasive. Throughout the book, we shall give many real-world examples of social dilemma situations. Social psychology is sometimes criticized for studying abstract questions that have little relevance to society. By contrast, many of the findings we shall report (derived from laboratory experimentation) are directly adaptable to real-life dilemmas. This is not to say that the techniques designed to improve cooperation (discussed in this book) can be easily implemented in the real world; however, it would certainly be possible to test some of them in an actual dilemma setting. The study of social dilemmas thus has ecological as well as theoretical relevance.

The first portion of the book (chapters 1–4) is organized historically. After a general introduction to social dilemmas in Chapter 1, we describe research with the prisoner's dilemma and its variants; progress to public goods; and then discuss social traps. In the next two substantive chapters, we discuss alternative approaches to the study of social dilemma behavior: Chapter 5 addresses the role of personality in social dilemmas, and Chapter 6 describes political science, economic, and biological approaches to the topic.

A project of this magnitude inevitably requires the help of others, and many individuals graciously offered their time and effort. Norbert Kerr and Scott Plous provided references and comments; members of the Social Dilemma Research Group (especially Lorne Hulbert) of the University of Illinois critiqued earlier versions of several chapters; and Jane Weber provided the clerical support necessary to pull all of the material together.

We would also like to thank those reviewers whose in-depth critiques directed us in completing the final version of this text: Scott Allison, University of Richmond; Charles Samuelson, Texas A & M University; and David Schroeder, University of Arkansas.

Introduction

A pervasive feature of social interaction is the conflict between an individual's motive to maximize personal (selfish) interests and the motive to maximize collective interests. Yet, in many situations, if all attempt to maximize their selfish interests, all are worse than if all cooperate to maximize their collective interests. Such conflicts are of interest to a variety of social scientists and this book will examine theory and research on how people are likely to resolve such conflicts of motives.

There are many real-life examples of such conflicts. Consider two examples described by Dawes (1980).

> "People asked to keep their thermostats low to conserve energy are being asked to suffer from the cold without appreciably conserving the fuel supply by their individual sacrifices; yet if all keep their thermostats high, all may run out of fuel and freeze. . . .
>   Women in India will almost certainly outlive their husbands, and for the vast majority who can't work, their only source of support in their old age is their male sons. Thus each individual woman

achieves the highest social payoff by having as many children as possible. Yet the resulting overpopulation makes a social security or old-age benefit system impossible, so that all the women are worse off than they would have been if they had all practiced restraint in having children'' (p. 171).

To demonstrate how frequently such conflicts occur, consider the following examples:

- In Los Angeles, residents are asked to help reduce air pollution by car-pooling, using public transportation, bicycling, or walking, instead of driving a car. For many people, such measures are an inconvenience, and any single person's ability to affect air quality is negligible. Yet if no one does this, all residents will breathe dirty air.
- Every Labor Day weekend, the Muscular Dystrophy Association holds its annual telethon to raise money. Since it is highly unlikely that any one person will ever need the charity's services, that person will be giving money for a service he/she will probably never use. If no one sends money, though, the charity cannot survive, and society will have in its midst a deadly affliction that is not being fought.

We could list many more examples, but these should be sufficient to illustrate our point: *Social dilemmas* are faced by most people on a regular basis. (The reader interested in more examples should see Cross and Guyer, 1980.)

Buchanan and Tullock (1962) imply that one of the main functions of government is to regulate and inhibit the selfish behavior of individuals in social dilemmas. Buchanan and Tullock assume that cooperation is necessary for collective survival. Yet, how can cooperation develop in a world of people who seek their own personal advantage and interest? The most famous and pessimistic answer to this question was given by Thomas Hobbes (1651/1939), the famous seventeenth-century philosopher, in his treatise on government, *Leviathan*. Hobbes argued that before the existence of government, society consisted of selfish individuals who competed ruthlessly with each other. As a result, life was ''. . . solitary, poor, nasty, brutish, and short'' (Hobbes, 1651/1939, p. 100). A strong central authority and government was necessary, according to Hobbes, to enforce cooperation on these ruthlessly competing individuals and to transform the state of nature to the state of society. Is it possible for humans to develop or evolve a cooperative society without such a central authority? It is this question that is at the heart of this book. What can be done to encourge people to be more cooperative? Throughout this text, we will describe laboratory studies of social dilemmas and discuss what implications these studies may have for real-life social dilemmas.

The Nature of Interdependence

Before we present a more rigorous definition of a social dilemma, it will be necessary to examine social situations at a more general level. It will also be desirable to describe research on social dilemmas in the context of theoretical orientations in social psychology. For this purpose, we shall emphasize a class of theories called "social exchange." Theories of social exchange assume that all social interaction involves a bargaining relationship in which people exchange rewards and costs (punishments). For example, in many families the husband may agree to mow the lawn and shovel snow, while the wife may agree to cook and wash the dishes. In other families, the husband dislikes mowing the lawn and may prefer to cook; hence, they may agree to share these duties. But in either case, rewards and costs are involved in the relationship. A fundamental assumption of exchange theories is that people are motivated to maximize rewards and minimize costs, where rewards are anything that humans desire (money, status, power, etc.) and costs are anything that humans wish to avoid (loss of self-esteem, anxiety, guilt, etc.).

Although there are several theorists who are associated with theories of social exchange (Thibaut and Kelley, 1959; Homans, 1961; Blau, 1964), we shall focus on the theory proposed by Thibaut and Kelley (1959) because their formulation is particularly appropriate for the analysis of social dilemma behavior. According to Thibaut and Kelley, social interaction can be described with a *matrix* (or table) *of outcomes.* To illustrate the nature of interdependence with outcome matrices, let us see what a matrix would look like in a simple case of two-person interaction. In the two-person case, the rows of an outcome matrix represent all possible actions of Person A. Each row corresponds to one of many possible behaviors Person A may choose. Conversely, the columns represent all possible actions of Person B. The entries in the cells of the matrix, corresponding to the intersections of rows and columns, represent the outcomes of the two persons. Thus, an outcome matrix describes the outcomes that would result from all possible combinations of behaviors that Persons A and B could engage in.

TABLE 1.1 A Sample Interaction Matrix of Outcomes

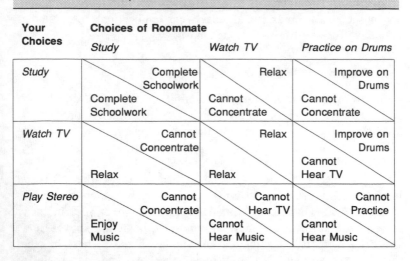

Your Choices	Choices of Roommate		
	Study	Watch TV	Practice on Drums
Study	Complete Schoolwork / Complete Schoolwork	Relax / Cannot Concentrate	Improve on Drums / Cannot Concentrate
Watch TV	Cannot Concentrate / Relax	Relax / Relax	Improve on Drums / Cannot Hear TV
Play Stereo	Cannot Concentrate / Enjoy Music	Cannot Hear TV / Cannot Hear Music	Cannot Practice / Cannot Hear Music

For example, consider the matrix in Table 1.1. This matrix represents a simplified type of interdependency between you and your roommate. Let's assume that, in this instance, each of you may engage in one of three behaviors. (Of course, in real life your set of possible behaviors would be much larger.) You could study, watch television, or listen to your stereo. Your roommate could study, watch television, or practice the drums. Table 1.1 shows outcomes that might result from each combination of these behaviors. (Your outcomes fall below the diagonal lines, your roommate's above the diagonals.) As you can see, some combinations produce positive outcomes for both of you; some produce positive outcomes for only one of you; and some produce negative outcomes for both.

Correspondence of Outcomes

Consider what is likely to happen if the same combination of behaviors that produces a good outcome for you yields a poor outcome for the other person. The extent to which the two sets of outcomes are similar is referred to as *correspondence of outcomes* (Kelley and Thibaut, 1978). Kelley and Thibaut (1978) have developed a mathematical index (a formula) to measure the degree of correspondence of outcomes, and all types of 2×2 matrices can be classified according to this index. More importantly, this index can be used to predict the nature of the interaction (cooperation or competition) between the two parties that are involved.

Consider the three outcome matrices shown in Table 1.2. In the matrix shown in Table 1.2a, the *sum* of the outcomes in each cell is zero; hence, this type of situation is frequently called a *zero-sum game*. A positive outcome for one person will necessarily produce a negative outcome for the other person. A wager between two persons is an example of a zero-sum game. According to Thibaut and Kelley, the zero-sum game represents an extreme situation in which outcomes are completely *noncorrespondent*. The zero-sum game is a purely competitive situation because what one person gains the other must lose. This idea is consistent with the definition of a competitive situation as one in which the goals of the two parties are mutually incompatible (Deutsch, 1949). In contrast, in the game shown in Table 1.2b, the *difference* between the outcomes in each cell is zero: what one person gains the other must also gain and what one person loses, the other must lose. An example here would be a team sport. If a baseball player hits four home runs in a game, and the final score is 4 to 0, then his entire team wins; his teammates cannot be given a loss simply because they did not score any runs. Similarly, if the final score is 6 to 4, he cannot be given a win simply because he played so well. He loses along with his team. This represents the extreme form of *correspondence of outcomes*. Hence, this is a purely cooperative situation because the goals of the two persons are mutually compatible (Deutsch, 1949).

From a social psychological perspective, the purely competitive and purely cooperative situations are not interesting because behavior in these situations do not provide much information about what variables affect cooperative and competitive behavior. For example, suppose we inform two subjects that their task is to maximize gain, and ask them to make choices in the cooperative game of Table 1.2b. If we find that they cooperated and chose A_1 and B_1, we would not be too surprised. Indeed, the interesting result is the case where they did *not* cooperate and chose A_2, B_2. But in this case, since they did not maximize gain, we would conclude that either the subjects were not motivated to maximize gain, or they did not understand the experimenter's instructions. Thus, the results would not be particularly interesting or important no matter how the subjects behaved.

The pure cases of cooperative and competitive interdependence are important from a general theoretical perspective, and according to Kelley and Thibaut (1968) such pure cases rarely occur in real life. For example, an extreme form of competitive interdependence is war. But even war between nations is not a purely competitive (zero-sum) situation, because both sides can lose and

TABLE 1.2 Three Types of Outcome Interdependence. Lower-left and upper-right entries in each cell of choice matrix represent outcomes of person A (row) and person B (column), respectively.

a. Zero-Sum Matrix

Choices of A	Choices of B — B_1	Choices of B — B_2
A_1	5 / −5	−8 / 8
A_2	8 / −8	−2 / 2

b. Zero-Difference Matrix

Choices of A	Choices of B — B_1	Choices of B — B_2
A_1	5 / 5	8 / 8
A_2	−8 / −8	−2 / −2

c. Mixed-Motive Matrix

Choices of A	Choices of B — B_1	Choices of B — B_2
A_1	5 / 5	−8 / 8
A_2	8 / −8	−2 / −2

nations often abide by certain rules, e.g., prohibitions against poison gas, or humane treatment of prisoners of war. Conversely, an extreme case of cooperative interdependence is the interaction among members of a basketball team. Even though the goal of all members is to win the game, some members may score more than others, some may play a better game than others, and some may not get to play at all. The important point is that the difference in outcomes in all cases is not zero; hence, it is not a purely cooperative situation.

The Mixed-Motive Case

The vast majority of research using outcome matrices have been based on mixed-motive games, i.e., situations that are neither purely competitive nor purely cooperative. The term *mixed-motive game* was first introduced by Schelling (1960), an economist, to refer to situations in which an individual is faced with a conflict between the motive to compete and the motive to cooperate. To illustrate the mixed-motive case, consider the two-person prisoner's dilemma, a parable that represents the essence of this conflict of motives, as shown in Table 1.2c. In the prisoner's dilemma, two prisoners are accused of being partners in a crime. They are in separate cells and unable to communicate with each other. The district attorney approaches each prisoner separately with the same proposal. If the prisoner will "turn state's evidence" and testify against his partner, he will go free and his partner will receive a long sentence. However, if both turn state's evidence, both will receive an intermediate sentence. If neither prisoner turns state's evidence, both will receive a short sentence. Each prisoner must make his decision whether to turn state's evidence (defect from his partner) or refuse to turn state's evidence (cooperate with his partner), without knowing the other's decision.

Each prisoner would prefer to go free (if he defects and the other prisoner cooperates) over a short sentence (if both cooperate), and would prefer a short sentence over a long sentence (if both defect). Moreover, each prisoner knows that the other prisoner has the same preferences. If we denote the two prisoners as A and B, consider the reasoning of prisoner A. If the other prisoner (B) defects, A is also better off defecting. If prisoner B does not defect, A is better off defecting. Thus, A should defect. Prisoner B will also reason the same way. Thus, regardless of the choice of the other, each should defect. But if both defect, both will be worse off than if both cooperate. The dilemma is based on the fact that individual rationality has led to collectively irrational behavior. By pursuing their own selfish interests, each is worse off. If each could trust the other to cooperate, both would be better off.

Game theorists have formalized the situation represented by the prisoner's dilemma in a two by two (two-person, two-choice) matrix (see Table 1.2c). The two rows (A_1 and A_2) are the possible actions for the first person: to cooperate with his partner (A_1: not turn state's evidence) or to defect from his partner (A_2: turn state's evidence). The two columns (B_1 and B_2) are two possible actions for the second person. The joint choices of the two possible actions result in four possible outcome cells, as shown in Table 1.2c. The consequences or payoffs for each of the two players in the four cells may be summarized as follows: (a) If both cooperate (A_1 and B_1), each receives +5; (b) If both defect (A_2 and B_2), each receives −2; and (c) If one cooperates and one defects (A_1, B_2) or (A_2, B_1), the defector receives +8 and the cooperator receives −8. Thus, each is tempted to defect, but if both succumb to this temptation, both are worse off (−2, −2) than if they trusted each other and cooperated (+5, +5). Thus, the two persons are faced with the conflict between maximizing individual interests (defect) and maximizing collective welfare (cooperate). In addition to the prisoner's dilemma, there are many types of mixed-motive situations that vary considerably in the intensity of the mixed-motive conflict. The prisoner's dilemma is unique in that the conflict is most intense.

Social Dilemmas

A general definition of a social dilemma is a situation in which a group of N-persons ($N \geq 2$) must choose between maximizing selfish interests and maximizing collective interests. It is generally more profitable for each person to maximize selfish interests but if all choose to maximize selfish interests, all are worse off than if all choose to maximize collective interests. This definition is more general than the definition proposed by Dawes (1980), but it is consistent with the definition proposed by Liebrand (1983) and with the generic problem of collective dilemmas described by Schelling (1978).[1]

Many social scientists are interested in social dilemmas and different labels have been used to describe such situations, for example, "the tragedy of the commons" (Hardin, 1968), "the commons dilemma" (Dawes, 1975), "social traps" (Platt, 1973), "the free-rider problem" (Olson, 1965), and "multiple prisoner's dilemma" (Schelling, 1973). Since there are many real-life situations that satisfy the conditions of a social dilemma, not surprisingly, a variety of experimental paradigms have been proposed to simulate such

TABLE 1.3 Example of a Five-person Prisoner's Dilemma Game[a]

Choice of S[b]	Number of Others Choosing C				
	0	1	2	3	4
D	2	4	6	8	10
C	0	2	4	6	8

[a]S denotes person S, one of the five members of the group.
[b]C and D denote cooperative and defecting choices, respectively.

situations. In this book we shall restrict ourselves to three basic prototypes: (1) the prisoner's dilemma, (2) the social trap analog, and (3) the public goods paradigm.

The Prisoner's Dilemma

The two-person prisoner's dilemma, as we indicated earlier, is a special case of a social dilemma. The extension of the two-person prisoner's dilemma to the case of larger groups, hereafter called the N-person prisoner's dilemma (N > 2), is also a special case. Table 1.3 shows an example of a five-person prisoner's dilemma, where C and D represent the cooperative and defecting choices, respectively. The entries denote the outcomes for person S, one of the five persons in the group. For example, if person S chooses C and the other four also choose C, all would receive 8 points (outcome in row C under column 4). If person S chooses D and the other four persons also choose D, then all receive 2 points (outcome in row D under column 0). Thus, all are better off if all choose C (8 points) than if all choose D (2 points). But note that no matter how many others choose C, the outcome for the D-choice is greater than for the C-choice. Thus, this game satisfies the general conditions of the social dilemma.

Social Traps

Another important class of social dilemmas is called a social trap (Platt, 1973; Cross and Guyer, 1980). A *social trap* can be characterized as a situation in which the behavior of organisms yields two outcomes: a small positive outcome that is immediate and a large negative outcome that is delayed. A special case of a social trap is the "replenishable resource trap" (Messick and Brewer, 1983), which simulates a situation in which there is a common resource pool from which individuals can "harvest" resources from the common pool.

The pool replenishes itself at a predetermined rate, but if the members "overharvest" from the pool (extract resources faster than the replenishment rate), the pool can become "extinct." Thus, the members must somehow coordinate their harvesting behavior so that the common pool will not be depleted.

There are hundreds of examples of social traps, e.g., industrial air pollution, which leads to acid rain and the destruction of lakes, or "over-harvesting" of whales to extinction. Consider Garrett Hardin's (1968) description of the "Tragedy of the Commons." A "commons" is a good or resource that is publicly owned and is freely accessible to the public, e.g., public parks, beaches, and libraries are commons. In Hardin's example, the Commons was a public pasture, such as in the old New England villages, where herdsmen could graze their cows freely. Each herdsman, seeking to maximize profit, rationally increases his herd size. What is the harm in adding one or two more animals? But there is an upper limit on the number of animals that can be sustained by the common pasture. If a large number of herdsmen increase their herd size, the common pasture cannot be sustained because the amount of grazing will exceed the replenishment rate of the pasture. Of course, the commons is ultimately destroyed by overgrazing, resulting in the loss of the entire herd that grazed on it.

The essential condition of a social trap is when ". . . each individual . . . continues to do something for his individual advantage that collectively is damaging to the group as a whole" (Platt, 1973, p. 1). In terms of the general conditions of a social dilemma, the defecting choice is to obtain immediate gratification, while the cooperative choice is to refrain from seeking the immediate positive outcome, and thus avoid the long term negative consequence. It is called a social trap (Platt, 1973) because it simulates a situation in which an organism (fish, animal, etc.) is faced with a choice between satisfying its hunger by entering a trap set by a hunter, or foregoing immediate gratification of its hunger. If it succumbs to the temptation of the bait set by the hunter, the long-term negative consequence is its loss of freedom (capture by the hunter).

The Public Goods Paradigm

The third major type of social dilemma is the problem of providing a public good, such as parks, schools, mass transit, etc. A *public good* is a commodity or service that can be easily supplied to all members of a group (community, society). Furthermore, once provided, no member can be excluded from its consumption or use (Barry and Hardin, 1982). As the term implies, the public goods paradigm simulates a situation in which members of a community must contribute money, taxes, effort, etc., to provide a public good that is shared equally by the members, regardless of their contributions. The dilemma is based on the belief that others will make sufficient contributions and one can "free ride" (Olson, 1965); however, if everyone attempts to be a free rider, the bonus will not be provided, and everyone will be worse off.

As in the case of a social trap, the public goods paradigm involves two types of outcomes: a short-term and a delayed outcome. However, the size and reinforcement of these outcomes (reward vs. punishment) are reversed. Unlike the social trap, the short-term outcome is small and negative (e.g., contribution of money or effort), and the delayed outcome is large and positive (provision of the public good). Platt (1973) and his collaborators, Cross and Guyer (1980), distinguish between a "trap" and a "fence." In a *trap,* the short-run reinforcement is positive and the long-run consequence is negative; in a *fence* (or countertrap), the reward and punishment are reversed: the short-run reinforcement is negative and the long-run consequence is positive. Thus, the public goods paradigm represents a fence, whereas the replenishable resource paradigm represents a trap. The two classes of dilemmas are depicted as follows (Platt, 1973):

Social Trap	*Social Fence*
B	B
S R_S^+ . . . R_L^-	S R_S^- . . . R_L^+

where S denotes a social dilemma (stimulus) situation;
R_S denotes short-run reinforcement for the individual;
R_L denotes long-run reinforcement for the group; and
R^+ and R^- denote positive and negative reinforcement, respectively; and B denotes behavior.

Both Platt (1973) and Cross and Guyer (1980) claim that social traps and fences are insidious because of the importance of the delayed consequence. From studies of operant conditioning (cf. Skinner, 1953), we know that immediate reinforcement has much greater impact on behavior, and the longer the delay of reinforcement, the less the effect on behavior. In many real-life social dilemmas, especially social traps, the delay is so long that once we realize the enormity of the consequences, it may be too late to recover from our mistakes. Examples of this problem include depletion of the ozone layer in the upper atmosphere from the use of fluorocarbons, and the "greenhouse effect" from the use of fossil fuels.

Take-Some and Give-Some Games

At this point we shall describe another important class of games called give-some and take-some games, first proposed by Hamburger (1973). These games are important because they are basic prototypes of the social trap and public good paradigms, and they also can be represented as a prisoner's dilemma. Hamburger's definitions of the two types of games leads to some complications that are beyond the scope of this book.[2] Consequently, for the purpose of simplifying the presentation, we shall adopt a reconceptualization of these games proposed by Dawes (1980).

According to Dawes' (1980) formulation, in a *take-some game* each member of the group is told that those who choose D will receive $X; those who choose C will each receive $Y. X is greater than Y so that it is individually rational to choose D. But all are informed that for each person who chooses D, all will be penalized $Z (a negative externality).[3] Consequently, if all choose D, all receive a smaller payoff than if all choose C, thus satisfying the conditions of a social dilemma.

Dawes (1980) gives the following example. In a three-person game, each player who chooses D (by holding up a red chip) receives $3, but each of the three players is fined $1 for each person who chooses D. Each player who chooses C (by holding up a blue chip) receives $1 but with no fine (penalty). This game is defined as follows: X = $3, Y = $1, and Z = –$1. Table 1.4a shows the outcome matrix for this game. For example, suppose all three choose D. Each will receive $3 but each will be fined $3 ($1 for each D-choice), resulting in zero payoff. If all choose C, each will receive $1 but with no penalty, resulting in the outcome of $1 each. It can be seen that no matter how many of the others choose C, the D-choice yields a higher payoff than the C-choice. But if all choose D, all are worse off (payoff of 0) than if all choose C (payoff of $1). Thus, this game satisfies the conditions of a social dilemma.

In the *give-some game,* the externality (Z) is positive in value, and each person is *rewarded $Z for each person who chooses C.* Consider Dawes' (1980) example for a five-person game. Each of

TABLE 1.4 Outcome Matrices for Take-Some and Give-Some
Games (from Dawes, 1980)

a. Three-Person Take-Some Game

	Number of Others Choosing C		
	0	1	2
D	0	1	2
C	−1	0	1

b. Five-Person Give-Some Game

	Number of Others Who Choose C				
	0	1	2	3	4
D	8	11	14	17	20
C	0	3	6	9	12

five players may keep $8 (the D-choice) or give $3 to each of the
others (the C-choice). If all choose D, each receives $8, but if all
choose C, each receives $12 (4 × $3). This game is defined as follows: $X = \$8$, $Y = 0$, and $Z = \$3$. Table 1.4b shows the outcome
matrix for this game. Again, it can be seen that the D-choice yields
a higher payoff than the C-choice, but if all choose D (payoff of
$8), all are worse off than if all choose C (payoff of $12).

The take-some and give-some games are basic prototypes of
the social trap and public goods dilemmas. Overconsumption of a
replenishable resource or polluting the environment are special
cases of a social trap, and the take-some game simulates such problems because all members of society are penalized (fined $Z) when
anyone kills an endangered animal or pollutes the environment. Cor-
respondingly, the give-some game simulates a public goods dilemma because all of us benefit a small amount when we pay our
taxes, give to charity, or volunteer our services for nonprofit organizations. In subsequent chapters of this book, we shall examine such
real-life dilemmas in much greater detail.

Summary and Conclusions

Social dilemmas are very pervasive and many real-life examples of social dilemmas were described. Several distinct methods have been used to study social dilemmas, but in this book we shall emphasize a method (or approach) developed by Thibaut and Kelley (1959) called "exchange theory." Their approach is based on analyzing social behavior in terms of a matrix (or table) of outcomes. A highly simplified outcome matrix involves two persons, each with two choices, referred to as a 2×2 game. The 2×2 game is a basic prototype of many real-life situations and they have been used to study cooperative and competitive behavior.

We described three basic research paradigms that have been used to simulate social dilemmas: (1) the prisoner's dilemma game, (2) the social trap or replenishable resource trap, and (3) the provision of a public good. The remainder of this book will be devoted to summaries of theory and research on the three main types of social dilemmas.

In the remaining chapters of this book we shall also focus on factors that affect cooperative behavior in various types of social dilemmas, and suggest ways of facilitating cooperative behaviors. We shall look first at the *prisoner's dilemma*. This deceptively simple game and its variant, the *N-person dilemma*, has inspired hundreds of studies since its introduction in the 1950s, including some studies by researchers in such diverse disciplines as mathematics, biology, and political science. Next, we shall examine the *public goods* paradigm, an old problem in economics that has only recently caught the attention of psychologists. Finally, we shall discuss the general class of *social traps*, focusing specifically on *resource dilemmas*, a current real-world issue that demands the attention of researchers.

Notes

1. Dawes' (1980) definition is more restrictive than our definition, and some interesting types of dilemmas (e.g., Chicken and step-level public goods) do not meet the conditions specified by his definition. Schelling's (1978) definition is more general and according to his conceptualization, the prisoner's dilemma is only one of many types of collective dilemmas. His general definition includes, ". . . all the situations in which equilibria achieved by unconcerted or undisciplined action are inefficient—the situations in which everybody could be better off, or some collective total could be made larger, by concerted or disciplined or organized or regulated or centralized decisions." (p. 225). Liebrand's (1983) definition is also more general and includes games of Chicken and other "nontrivial" dilemma games.

2. In Hamburger's conceptualization of these games, the outcomes in a give-some game are deterministic, whereas the outcomes in a take-some game are probabilistic and involve an element of chance. Moreover, Hamburger shows that the two types of games are not comparable because in a give-some game the slopes of the payoff functions for the two choices are always equal (see Fig. 2.2), whereas in the take-some game the slope of the function for the D-choice is greater than for the C-choice ("greed" is greater than "fear").

3. An externality is an economic concept that refers to a side effect of a firm's actions that does not enter into the firm's profits (or losses), but has consequences for people outside of (external to) the firm. For example, if a manufacturer pollutes the air and this action is unregulated, it is a negative externality because other people (external to the firm) are affected by the pollution. In the case of a positive externality, if a manufacturer builds a new plant in a given area, property values in the surrounding area may increase dramatically. Of course, the increased noise and traffic congestion is a negative externality.

CHAPTER

2

The Prisoner's Dilemma

In the previous chapter we defined a social dilemma as a situation in which: (1) two or more individuals can behave so as to maximize personal interests or maximize collective interests, but (2) if all behave so as to maximize personal interests all are worse off than if all behave so as to maximize collective interests. In this chapter we shall present theory and research on a special case of a social dilemma called the prisoner's dilemma.

Most people are familiar with the two-person prisoner's dilemma game but few are acquainted with the N-person case (N ≥ 3). This is unfortunate because the N-person case has greater generality and applicability to real-life situations, and is considered to be a prototype of many critical problems facing society. The prisoner's dilemma must satisfy some restrictive conditions; hence, we shall first present the simple two-person case and then return to the N-person case later in the chapter.

The Two-Person Prisoner's Dilemma

In the two-person prisoner's dilemma, hereafter denoted PDG, each person has two choices, a C-choice (cooperation) and a D-choice (defection), as shown in Tables 2.1a and 2.1b. In each cell of these outcome matrices, the value in the lower left denotes the outcome for Person 1, and the value in the upper right denotes the outcome for Person 2. Table 2.1a shows one example of a PDG and Table 2.1b shows a general (abstract) representation of the PDG. The labels R, P, T, and S are interpreted as follows (Rapoport and Chammah, 1965): R denotes the *reward* for mutual cooperation; P denotes the *punishment* for mutual defection; T denotes

---

TABLE 2.1 Outcome Matrices for the Prisoner's Dilemma Game

a. Example of Prisoner's Dilemma

Choices of Person 1	Choices of Person 2	
	C	D
C	5 / 5	0 / −8
D	−8 / 8	−2 / −2

b. General Prisoner's Dilemma

Choices of Person 1	Choices of Person 2	
	C	D
C	R / R	T / S
D	S / T	P / P

temptation to defect (assuming both have cooperated); and S denotes the *"sucker's payoff,"* the consequence of being double-crossed after making the cooperative choice. The main restrictions of the prisoner's dilemma game are that $T > R > P > S$. These restrictions may be summarized and interpreted in terms of three motivational tendencies: (a) the quantity $(T - R)$ represents "greed," the motive to defect to obtain T, rather than to settle for R, the outcome for mutual cooperation; (b) the quantity $(R - P)$ represents the incentive to obtain R through mutual cooperation and avoid P, the outcome for mutual defection; and (c) the quantity $(P - S)$ represents "fear" of the sucker's payoff if one's trust in the other is betrayed.

If any of these inequalities $(T > R > P > S)$ are violated, the nature of the conflict between maximizing individual and collective interests may be drastically altered. For example, if $R = P$, and both choose D, their joint outcome will be the same as their joint outcome if they both chose C. Thus, the principles of individual and collective rationality will not be in conflict. Similarly, if $T = R$ and $P = S$, there would be no temptation to defect and no fear of the sucker's payoff.

If the game is iterated (played for many trials), a second restriction is also necessary: $2R > (T + S)$. If $(T + S)$ is greater than 2R, it would be optimal for the two players to alternate between the (C, D), and (D, C) outcomes, instead of choosing C on all trials; thus, they would be cooperating if they chose C on 50 percent of the trials. In contrast, if 2R is greater than $(T + S)$, it would be optimal to choose C on all trials, and this is the definition of mutual cooperation. For example, suppose we change the value of T in the game depicted in Table 2.1a from 8 to 20. Then, 2R (5 + 5) is less than $T + S$ (20 – 8). If the game is played for 100 trials, the two players may alternate between the (C, D) and (D, C) outcomes, and they would receive –8 on 50 trials and +20 on 50 trials, for a total of 600 points. The average payoff over the 100 trials would be 6 points per trial and this would be greater than the average of 5 points per trial if they had made the C-choice on all trials. Thus, if 2R is less than $(T + S)$, we would not be able to unambiguously define mutual cooperation because alternation between the C and D-choices, as well as 100 percent C-choices, could be interpreted as mutual cooperation.

The unique feature of the PDG is that two basic axioms of rational choice are in conflict. The first axiom is based on the concept of *dominance of choices*. Given two choices, X and Y,

TABLE 2.2 Outcome Matrix in Which One Choice (X) Dominates Another (Y)

All Possible Events

Choices	1	2	3	4	5	6	7
X	2	8	6	5	3	4	2
Y	0	1	4	-1	-2	1	-4

X dominates Y if the outcome for X is greater than the outcome for Y for all possible events that can occur. To illustrate this principle, consider the outcome matrix shown in Table 2.2; for example, the outcomes may depend on the occurrence of some natural event such as the roll of a die, who wins the World Series in baseball, or the choice of another person. It can be seen that the outcome for Choice X is greater than for Choice Y for all possible events that can occur. Given that one choice dominates another, one of the axioms of rational choice prescribes that one should choose the dominating choice (Choice X in this example).

The basic dilemma is based on the conflict between the principle of dominance, an axiom of *individual rationality,* and the principle of "Pareto optimality," an axiom of *collective rationality.* A joint outcome, resulting from the choices of two (or more) players, is said to be *Pareto optimal* if there is no other outcome that is greater for both (or all) players simultaneously. The principle of Pareto optimality states that it is not collectively rational for a group of persons to make choices in which everyone could have obtained a greater outcome from another set of choices.

For the PDG shown in Table 2.1a consider the outcome for Person 1, the row player. Note that no matter what Person 2 chooses, the outcome for Choice D is greater than the outcome for Choice C. If Person 2 chooses C, the outcome of 8 is greater than 5, and if Person 2 chooses D, the outcome of -2 is greater than -8. Thus the D-choice dominates the C-choice, and Person 1 should choose D. Since this is a symmetric game (the pattern of outcomes is identical for two players), the D-choice dominates the C-choice for Person 2 as well, and the principle of dominance prescribes that both should choose D. If both conform to this principle of rational choice, the outcome for each player will be -2. However, the (D, D) outcome of (-2 -2) is not Pareto optimal because the (C, C) outcome of (5, 5) is better for both players. Thus, the unique property of the PDG is that the players are faced with the conflict between maximizing personal gain, based on individual rationality, and maximizing joint gain, based on collective rationality.

The Win-Stay, Lose-Change Principle

According to exchange theory (Kelley and Thibaut. 1959; Homans, 1960), an individual is likely to repeat behaviors that have been rewarded in the past, and avoid behaviors that have been punished. This phenomenon is known as the "win-stay, lose-change" principle. Let us demonstrate this principle using the prisoner's dilemma in Table 2.1a. There are four patterns of choices that are possible on the first trial: CC, CD, DC, and DD. (Assume that choices are made simultaneously, so that one person cannot wait and observe the other's choice before acting.) Most people would consider a positive outcome (in this case, $R = 5$ and $T = 8$) to be a reward, and a negative outcome ($P = -2$ and $S = -8$) to be a punishment. If the pattern of choices on trial 1 is DD, then both players will receive a punishment (-2), and both should change behaviors on the next trial. Thus, on trial 2, both players will switch from D to C, the pattern of choice will be CC, both players will get a reward ($+5$), and both will stay with this behavior on future trials. If the choice pattern on trial 1 is CD or DC, then the C-chooser will get a punishment (-8), and the D-chooser a reward ($+8$). On the next trial, the C-chooser will switch; the D-chooser will not. The result on trial 2 will be the choice pattern DD, which gives both players a punishment. Consequently, on trial 3 both will switch to C, both will get a reward for doing so, and both will continue to choose C on future trials. The inference is clear: the "win-stay, lose-change" principle predicts that, in a mixed-motive situation, two persons will achieve a mutually cooperative agreement.

We can demonstrate (theoretically) that "win-stay, lose-change" works. But do people really do this? Kelley, Thibaut, Radloff, and Mundy (1962) tested the principle within the context of a simple mixed-motive situation and found support for it: subjects often repeated a choice if it had been rewarded on the previous trial, but switched (change) from a choice that led to punishment.

With the prisoner's dilemma game, however, hundreds of studies have been conducted, and the results of these studies clearly do not support the principle. Most of these studies were conducted with college students who were separated so that they could not communicate with each other. They also played for very small incentives (e.g., 1 point = 1 cent). Studies also have been conducted using children, adults, groups of both sexes, and subjects from many different countries, and the results is almost always the same: the average proportion of cooperative choices is very low and rarely exceeds chance levels (.50). Now, what can account for this discrepancy between the prediction of the "win-stay, lose-change" rule and the observed behavior of subjects?

One plausible explanation for the discrepancy is that the subjects were not highly motivated because the incentives were trivial. If they had been given larger rewards (e.g., 1 point = 1 dollar), they would have cooperated more. However, studies that varied the size of the rewards have not produced consistent results; for example, one study that compared cooperation of subjects playing for pennies vs. playing for dollars produced no difference in proportion of cooperation (Knox and Douglas, 1971).

Another plausible explanation for this discrepancy is that the "win-stay, lose-change" rule ignores the expectations of the players, e.g., whether they trust each other (Deutsch, 1958, 1960 a & b), or the types of attributions they make about each other (Kelley and Stahelski, 1970a, 1970b). To illustrate this weakness of the "win-stay, lose-change" rule, suppose both players choose D on a given trial and receive outcomes of –2 each. We assumed earlier that this punishment would lead both to switch to the C-choice. However, it is also reasonable to assume that each might consider the expected consequence if one person switched and the other did not. It can be seen from the choice matrix of Table 2.1a that the person who switches will receive –8 while the person who does not switch will receive +8! Thus, if we consider the expectations of the players, there is an incentive *not* to switch from the (D, D) outcome. In other words, there may be two opposing motives in this situation. Although the negative outcomes should induce both subjects to switch, if one person switches and the other does not, the punishment will be much greater (–8). Moreover, if one repeats the choice and the other switches, the person who repeats will be rewarded (+8). Thus, Rapoport and Chammah (1965) have found that some pairs of subjects "lock-in" and remain in the (–2, –2) outcome for many trials. Most subjects however, manage to escape from this outcome, though not necessarily into the mutually cooperative (+5, +5) solution.

The mutually cooperative outcome suggests another example illustrating the effects of expectations. Suppose both players choose C on a given trial and receive +5 each. The "win-stay" rule predicts that this rewarding outcome should lead to repeated C-choices on all subsequent trials. But it is also reasonable to assume that one or both subjects might consider the expected outcome if one switched and the other did not. In this case, the person who switches (defects) receives +8 and the person who repeats the C-choice receives –8, sometimes called the "sucker's payoff." Thus, as in the case of mutual defection, there are two opposing motivational forces when both players make the C-choice: There is an incentive to repeat the C-choice, as predicted by the "win-stay" rule, and there is an opposing incentive to switch to the D-choice, either because of fear of the "sucker's payoff" (–8) or because of the temptation to obtain the +8 payoff. The main implication of these examples is that a person may not always repeat a choice that has been rewarded, or switch from a choice that has been punished.

This inconsistency in repeating or changing one's choice suggests another plausible explanation for the discrepancy between predicted and observed behavior. In deriving predictions from the "win-stay, lose-change" rule, we ignored the magnitude of the rewards and punishments, and assumed that the probability of repeating a choice, or switching from a previous choice, was 0 or 1. However, there is considerable evidence that choices in the prisoner's dilemma game (over trials) are rarely made in an "all or none" fashion, and are more likely to be probabilistic. Not surprisingly, the probability of a cooperative choice, as a function of outcomes on the previous trial, varies with the values of the outcome matrix (Rapoport and Chammah, 1965).

Despite this limitation of the "win-stay, lose-change" principle, additional support for this decision rule is provided by the results of studies in which the payoff values of the matrix are varied. A review of such studies by Wrightsman, O'Connor and Baker (1972) indicates that the likelihood of cooperation or competition is consistent with reinforcement principles.

Effects of Reward Structure

Consider the general case of the prisoner's dilemma game shown in Table 2.1b. There is considerable evidence (Rapoport and Chammah, 1965; Steele and Tedeschi, 1967) that the probability of a cooperative choice varies *directly* with the values of R and S, the two possible outcomes when a cooperative choice is made, and *inversely* with the values of T and P, the two possible outcomes when a competitive choice is made. With respect to the diagram of Table 2.1b, this implies that:

1. The greater the reward (R) for mutual cooperation (C, C), the greater the likelihood that it will be repeated;
2. The greater the punishment (P) for mutual defection (D, D), the greater the likelihood that it will *not* be repeated;
3. In the cases in which one person cooperates and one person defects (C, D or D, C): (a) The greater the punishment (S), *for a cooperative choice* that is not reciprocated, the greater the likelihood that it will *not* be repeated; and (b) The greater the reward (T) *for defection,* when the other cooperates, the greater the likelihood that it will be repeated.

Based on these effects, Rapoport (1967) proposed an *index of cooperation* for the prisoner's dilemma game, defined by Equation 2.1

$$K = \frac{R - P}{T - S} \qquad (2.1)$$

where K represents an index of cooperation, and T, R, P, and S represent the outcomes of the choice matrix, as shown in Table 2.1b.

Under the constraints of the prisoner's dilemma game, it can be shown that K varies between 0 and 1.0 (cannot be less than zero and cannot be greater than 1.0). For example, for the matrix of Table 2.1(a), $T = 8$, $R = 5$, $P = -2$, and $S = -8$, and $K = 7/16$ or .438. Hence, K is simply a number that varies between 0 and 1.0 ($0 < K < 1$), and the higher the value of K for a given choice matrix, the greater the level of cooperation that can be expected.

Table 2.3a shows the outcome matrix for the case when the reward for mutual cooperation (R) and the "sucker's payoff" (S) are increased in value, and the temptation to defect (T) and the punishment for mutual defection (P) are decreased in value. Compared with the outcomes in Table 2.1a, the value of K is much larger ($K = 30/32 = .94$), and a very high level of cooperation can be expected. Table 2.3b shows the outcomes for the opposite case when values of R and S are decreased, and values of T and P are increased. In this case, K is much smaller ($K = 2/80 = .025$), and a very low level of cooperation should be expected.

To illustrate the difference in incentives to cooperate in these games, let us consider how an individual might react to mutual defection. In Example 1 (high K), the two parties would receive −15

TABLE 2.3 Examples of Prisoner's Dilemmas with High and Low K-index Values[a]

a. Example 1: High K-index

Choices of Person 1	Choices of Person 2	
	C	D
C	15 \ 15	16 \ -16
D	-16 \ 16	-15 \ -15

b. Example 2: Low K-index

Choices of Person 1	Choices of Person 2	
	C	D
C	1 \ 1	40 \ -40
D	-40 \ 40	-1 \ -1

[a]Compared with the outcome values in the prisoner's dilemma in Table 2.1(a), in Example 1, the values of R and S [see table 2.1(b)] are larger, whereas the values of T and P are smaller. In Example 2, in contrast, the values of R and S are smaller and the values of T and P are larger.

each, but they would realize that they could have received +15 each if both had chosen C instead of D. Now, if one of them should switch to C on the next trial—to tacitly communicate a willingness to cooperate—it would involve a loss of only one point: an outcome of −16 (the sucker's payoff) instead of −15, if the D-choice is repeated. In contrast, how would the two parties react to mutual defection in Example 2 (low K)? In this case, they would receive −1 point each, but a switch to the C-choice would involve a loss of 39 points: −40 (sucker's payoff) instead of −1 for repeating the D-choice. Thus, neither party would be likely to choose C on the next trial to communicate an intent to cooperate. Moreover, note

TABLE 2.4 Example of Game of Chicken

	C (swerve)	D (straight)
C (swerve)	10 \ 10	20 \ −10
D (straight)	−10 \ 20	−20 \ −20

that the incentive to reach a mutually cooperative agreement (the CC-outcome) is also much smaller: outcome of +1 each instead of −1 each for the (D, D) outcome.

The main implication of these cases is that Rapoport's K-index is consistent with reinforcement theory: The greater the reward for the C-choice (values of R and S), and the smaller the rewards for the D-choice (values of T and P), the greater the cooperation. Moreover, there is considerable evidence to support the K-index, showing that cooperation varies directly with values of K (Rapoport & Chammah, 1965; Steele & Tedeschi, 1967).

The Game of Chicken

In addition to the PDG, other types of 2 × 2 games have been studied. Next to the PDG, the game that has received the greatest attention among social scientists is the game of CHICKEN. In terms of the symbols that we used to describe the PDG (see Table 2.1b), in CHICKEN the value of S is greater than P, whereas in the PDG, the value of P is greater than S; hence, CHICKEN is defined by the relations ($T > R > S > P$). Table 2.4 shows an example of CHICKEN. The game derives its name from the game teenagers play when they agree to drive their respective automobiles toward each other at great speed. Each has two choices: swerve to avoid a head-on collision or drive straight ahead. The mutually cooperative choice (swerving) yields the outcome R, and mutual noncooperation (driving straight ahead) yields the worst outcome (P). The dilemma is based on the fact that if one swerves and the other does not, the person who swerves is Chicken and receives a much lower outcome (S) than the person who does not swerve (outcome of T).

TABLE 2.5 Outcome Matrix of Cuban Missile Crisis

United States	Soviet Union	
	Withdraw	*Maintain*
Blockade	(3, 3) Compromise	(2, 4) Soviet Victory
Air Strike	(4, 2) U.S. Victory	(1, 1) Nuclear War

Note: First and second numbers in each cell represent outcomes for United States and Soviet Union, respectively.

The intensity of the conflict in CHICKEN is not as severe as in the PDG. Unlike the PDG (see Table 2.1a), Table 2.4 shows that the D-choice does not dominate the C-choice. The D-choice yields a higher outcome than C if the other person chooses C, but if the other chooses D, the outcome for the D-choice is less than for the C-choice. In other words, mutual defection yields the worst outcome for both parties and both are motivated to avoid mutual defection (DD-outcome). As one might expect, subjects cooperate more in CHICKEN than in the PDG, and the more severe the punishment for mutual defection, the greater the level of cooperation. Thus, some social scientists claim that CHICKEN provides a reasonable simulation of the "Cold War" relations between the United States and Russia shortly after World War II, where the outcome for mutual defection represents nuclear war between the two superpowers.

Table 2.5 shows one example of how CHICKEN can be used to model international relations. During the Cuban missile crisis of 1962, the United States discovered that the Soviets were installing medium and intermediate-range nuclear missiles in Cuba that could destroy a large number of cities in the U.S. The U.S. considered two alternative courses of action: (1) a naval blockade to prevent additional shipments of missiles, and (2) a "surgical" air strike to destroy the missiles already installed. The Soviets, in turn, also had two major options: (1) withdraw the missiles, or (2) maintain the missiles. Table 2.5 provides an analysis of the situation confronting the two countries, according to Brams (1975).

The probable outcomes are shown in each cell of the matrix and the numbers represent the relative (rank order) values of the four possible outcomes. It can be seen that the numbers conform to the pattern of outcomes defined by CHICKEN. The eventual outcome was a compromise resulting from the U.S. decision to blockade Cuba and the Soviet decision to withdraw the missiles. Obviously, both parties were highly motivated to avoid a nuclear war.

This analysis of the Cuban missile crisis is, of course, highly over-simplified. There were many other options that were considered by both sides, and there is no way to verify that the probable outcomes were valued as in the way depicted in Table 2.5. Moreover, the actions were not performed simultaneously by the two parties, but were performed sequentially. The U.S. first chose to blockade Cuba, and the Soviets had to choose between withdrawing or maintaining the missiles. Nonetheless, Brams argues that this analysis provides a reasonable simulation ("a skeletal picture") of the situation that confronted the two countries.

Some Factors That Affect Cooperation in the PDG

Choices of the Other Person

In addition to the effects of reward structure (values of T, R, P and S), there are several major factors that have been found to affect cooperation in the PDG. One important factor is information about the behavior and intentions of the other person. Given the pattern of outcomes in the PDG, it would be foolish to choose C (cooperate) if one did not expect the other person to reciprocate such behavior. To assess the effects of strategies (choices) of the other person on a subject's behavior, the experimenter must be able to systematically vary these strategies. For this purpose, two subjects are led to the experimental room and separated so that they cannot see or communicate with each other, and are led to believe they are playing the PDG with each other; in actuality, they are playing against a preprogrammed strategy used by the experimenter.

A review of studies based on this experimental paradigm (Oskamp, 1971; Wilson, 1973; Patchen, 1987) leads to the following conclusions: (1) an unconditional cooperative strategy (100 percent cooperation) is not effective in inducing subjects to cooperate; a person who cooperates unconditionally is likely to be exploited; (2) an unconditional competitive strategy also is not effective in inducing subjects to cooperate; not surprisingly, defection is likely to be met with defection; and (3) the most effective method of inducing subjects to cooperate is a conditional strategy in which the subject's choice on the previous trial is imitated on the next trial, called "tit-for-tat." We shall describe some important properties of this tit-for-tat strategy later in this chapter.

There are also some studies that varied the sequence of cooperative and competitive choices made by the "accomplice." For example, the results of a study by Harford and Solomon (1967) indicate that an initially competitive strategy—followed by a cooperative strategy—is more effective than an initial sequence of cooperative choices. There were two conditions in their study: In the Reformed Sinner condition, the accomplice defected on the first three trials ("sinned"), cooperated on the next three trials ("reformed"), and then played tit-for-tat for the next 20 test trials. In the Lapsed Saint condition, the accomplice cooperated on the first three trials ("Saint"), played tit-for-tat on the next three trials ("Lapsed"), and then continued with tit-for-tat on the next 20 test trials. On the 20 test trials in which the accomplice played tit-for-tat, the mean proportion of cooperative choices of the subjects was greater in the Reformed Sinner than in the Lapsed Saint condition.

Now why should the Reformed Sinner strategy evoke more cooperation than the Lapsed Saint strategy? One plausible reason for the effectiveness of the competition-then-cooperation (Reformed Sinner) sequence is that it leads to the perception that the other person is very "tough" and cannot be exploited. It may also give the impression that the other person has changed his/her intentions and is likely to reciprocate one's cooperative choices. The results for the Lapsed Saint condition may suggest that cooperative overtures (or any conciliatory moves)—if made early in the negotiations—may not be reciprocated. Indeed, such behavior may be perceived as a sign of weakness and attempts may be made to exploit the weakness. However, cooperative overtures may be very effective if they are made after being firm and unyielding; a conciliatory act by a "tough bargainer" is unexpected and incongruous and is likely to be quite salient, whereas a conciliatory act by a cooperative person ("a pacifist") is expected and may not be as salient.

Effects of Communication

Another important way to enhance cooperation in social dilemmas is to allow communication among the participants. Messick and Brewer (1983) suggest several reasons for the positive effect of communication: (1) communication provides information about the choices others are likely to make and introduces conformity pressures through the development of group norms: (2) discussion may enhance trust and reduce the perceived risk of making the cooperative choice; (3) communication may enhance the use of moral suasion to support collective goals; and (4) discussion may enhance group identity and cohesion among the members, thus increasing the motivation to maximize collective gain.

The results of earlier studies, however, (especially with the two-person PDG), did not show consistent effects of communication. Some studies showed that communication increased levels of cooperation, but several studies reported negligible effects. One reason for the discrepancy is that communication was not defined or manipulated in the same way in different studies. For example, in some studies face-to-face interaction was permitted, whereas in other studies subjects were asked to select messages to be sent from a predetermined set of messages prepared by the experimenter. Another reason is summarized by Terhune (1968), when he states that, ". . . it is not concluded that communication necessarily increases cooperation. Communication provides greater opportunity for cooperation, but that opportunity may either not be used, ineptly used, or used for deceit and vituperation." (1968, p. 22).

The results of a study by Dawes, McTavish and Shaklee (1977) are consistent with Terhune's conclusion. In the study by Dawes, et al., the effects of four levels of communication were compared: (1) no communication; (2) communication only about topics irrelevant to the game; (3) communication relevant to the game; and (4) relevant communication with nonbinding announcements of intended choices. The first two conditions evoked very low levels of cooperation (30 and 32 percent, respectively), while the last two conditions evoked very high levels (72 and 71 percent, respectively). Their results clearly indicate that it is discussion about the nature of the dilemma that enhances cooperation, and not the effects of getting to know one another through discussion of irrelevant matters.

The most striking effect of communication has been found in studies of the "minimal contributing set" (to be discussed in Chapter 3). When group members are allowed to discuss and designate those members who are to contribute to provide a public good, free riding is virtually eliminated (van de Kragt, et al., 1983) Their results are also consistent with Terhune's (1968) conclusions about the effects of communication. However, we shall postpone a detailed discussion of their study to a later chapter because it is based on the N-person social dilemma.

Individual Differences

Many attempts have been made to determine if cooperation in the PDG can be predicted with scores on personality scales. However, the results of such studies are very discouraging and the correlations between personality and cooperation are very low. When statistically significant correlations have been reported for a given scale, they have not been replicated in subsequent studies.

There are also many published studies reporting data on sex differences in the PDG. Some early studies reported that males were more cooperative than females, but some later studies report no sex differences, and a few studies found that females were more cooperative than males, thus contradicting the earlier results. Thus, despite the large number of studies of sex differences and cooperation in the PDG, the results are inconsistent and the underlying basis of the effect remains a mystery.

By far, the most promising approach to individual differences in cooperation are the results of studies originally conducted by Messick and McClintock (1968). They developed a method of measuring the motivational orientation of individuals and then validated their measures by predicting levels of cooperation on the basis of these measures. Three basic types of orientations (motives) were postulated: (1) the motive to maximize personal interests, denoted *maximize own gain;* (2) the motive to maximize both own as well as the other person's outcomes, denoted *maximize joint gain;* and (3) the motive to gain more than the other person, denoted *maximize relative gain.* According to their system, an individual can be classified on the basis of the relative importance of each type of motive. For example, for a cooperative person, maximizing joint gain is of primary importance, whereas for a competitive person, maximizing relative gain is of primary importance. For a person who is neither cooperative nor competitive (an individualistic orientation), maximizing own gain is of primary importance.

Subsequent research with Messick and McClintock's method of measuring motivational orientation provide considerable support for this approach. In Chapter 5 we shall describe the results of these studies on motivational orientation in detail.

Other Factors

There are several other factors that have been found to affect cooperation in the PDG. When subjects interact in a face-to-face situation, they are more cooperative than when they are separated and cannot see each other. One explanation for this effect is that in a face-to-face situation, subjects may engage in nonverbal communication (e.g., reacting with facial expressions after each trial), and as we shall see, permitting communication between the parties facilitates cooperation in different types of social dilemmas. A related factor is expectation of future interaction. If subjects are informed that they will be asked to interact on a subsequent task, they are likely to be more cooperative than when they do not expect to interact again.

Magnitude of incentives also have been found to affect cooperation but the results of different studies have been quite inconsistent. Some studies have found greater cooperation when the outcomes involve large amounts of money (e.g., playing for dollars) than when outcomes were trivial (e.g., playing for points or pennies). But the majority of studies report no significant difference in levels of cooperation when incentives are varied.

The results of a study by Knox and Douglas (1971) are typical. Using college students as subjects, pairs of students were asked to play the PDG for 10 trials. Half of them played for pennies and the other half played for dollars, with outcomes: $T = 5$, $R = 3$, $P = 1$, and $S = 0$. Thus, in the dollar condition, if two subjects cooperated on all 10 trials, they could have earned $30 each (in today's value of the dollar, $30 is worth about $75). Over the 10 trials, the average (median) proportions of cooperative choices for pennies and dollars were almost identical: 30 percent and 31 percent, respectively. One question that immediately can be raised is whether subjects in the dollar condition actually believed that they would be paid. Knox and Douglas considered this problem, and unlike the typical PDG experiment in which subjects are not awarded their earnings until the end of the experiment, subjects in their study were awarded their earnings after each trial.

Another interesting feature of their results is that they found a significant difference in the variance between the two conditions. The *variance* is a measure of variability in cooperation across pairs of subjects, and they found that variability was much larger in the dollar than in the penny condition. The variances were 7.34 and 25.50, for the penny and dollar conditions, respectively. This is an enormous difference in variability and implies that large incentives enhances the motivational tendencies of subjects *in both directions*. Whatever the tendency, large incentives magnify the tendency: cooperative pairs become more cooperative and competitive pairs become more competitive. This pattern of results (large difference in variance but no significant difference in average level of cooperation) has been replicated in a PDG study by Shaw (1976). These results suggest that the effects of incentives should interact with the K-index of the game: large incentives should enhance cooperation in a game with a large value of K, but should inhibit cooperation in a game with a small value of K.

Theoretical Interpretations of the Prisoner's Dilemma

One of the first experimental studies of the PDG was conducted by Morton Deutsch in 1958, and for the next ten to fifteen years an enormous number of PDG studies were conducted by a variety of social scientists. However, there was surprisingly little theoretical progress to explain cooperative behavior during this period. One important theoretical development is the measurement of social values. In addition, there have been four other important theoretical developments involving the PDG: (1) Kelley and Stahelski's (1970a, 1970b) attributional interpretation; (2) Kelley and Thibaut's (1978) theory of interdependence; (3) Pruitt and Kimmel's (1977) "goal/expectation" hypothesis; and (4) Axelrod's (1984) computer simulations.

An Attributional Approach

Kelley and Stahelski postulate that individuals can be classified as cooperators or competitors according to their goals (motives) in playing the PDG. They first classified a group of subjects as cooperators or competitors, according to responses to a questionnaire, and then asked pairs of subjects to play 40 trials of a PDG. There were three types of pairs: (1) cooperators paired with cooperators; (2) cooperators paired with competitors; and (3) competitors paired with competitors. After each block of 10 trials, subjects were asked about the goals and intentions of the other person, and they found that the inferences of cooperators were more accurate than those of competitors. Competitive persons perceived that others were uniformly competitive and competed against both competitive and cooperative persons. However, the perceptions of cooperative persons varied with the orientation of the other person, and they cooperated with cooperative persons but were competitive against competitive persons. Based on these results, Kelley and Stahelski hypothesized that cooperators see the world as consisting of people with both cooperative and competitive dispositions, whereas competitors see the world as consisting primarily of competitive people, like themselves.

TABLE 2.6 The Triangle Hypothesis

Own Orientation	Others Perceived To Be Cooperative . . .			Competitive
Cooperative	X	X	X	X
		X	X	X
. . .			X	X
Competitive				X

They called this hypothesis the "triangle hypothesis" because expectations form a triangle, as shown in Table 2.6. The first row of the table shows that the expectations of cooperative persons span the entire range from extremely cooperative to extremely competitive, and they believe others are heterogeneous in cooperativeness. In contrast, as we move toward the bottom row of the table, competitive persons expect others will be homogeneously (uniformly) competitive.

Kelley and Stahelski postulate that the triangle hypothesis is not restricted to the PDG and is applicable in a variety of social situations. There is considerable evidence to support the hypothesis in the PDG (e.g., Schlenker & Goldman, 1978; Maki & McClintock, 1983); however, some investigators have questioned the extent to which it can be generalized to other social situations (Miller & Holmes, 1975; Kuhlman & Wimberley, 1976). Nonetheless, one of the important implications of the triangle hypothesis is the self fulfilling aspect of the competitive person's stereotype of others. A competitive person expects others to compete, behaves competitively, and thus, induces others (both competitive and cooperative persons) to reciprocate such behavior.

A Theory of Interdependence

In the previous chapter we described Thibaut and Kelley's (1959) exchange theory of social interaction. As an extension of this theory, Kelley and Thibaut (1978) proposed an important distinction between two types of outcome matrices: the "given matrix" and the "effective matrix." The *given matrix* is the objective matrix of outcomes presented to the subject by the experimenter, whereas the *effective matrix* is the subjective matrix of outcomes as perceived or interpreted by the subject. Depending on individual differences in motivational orientations, individuals are assumed to transform the given matrix into the effective matrix. Kelley and Thibaut hypothesize that accurate predictions of behavior will not be possible from the given matrix alone, and we must first evaluate how individuals transform the given matrix to accurately predict behavior.

Kelley and Thibaut describe several types of transformations, but for the purpose of this chapter, we shall restrict our presentation to the outcome transformation. As the term implies, outcome transformations refer to subjective changes in the outcomes of social interaction. Kelley and Thibaut proposed three main types of outcome transformations: (1) transform so as to maximize the other person's outcome; (2) transform so as to maximize joint outcome; and (3) transform so as to maximize relative outcome.

To illustrate these transformations, consider the given matrix for the PDG shown in Figure 2.1, and the three effective matrices resulting from the three types of transformations. In each case, we assume that both players use the same transformation. As shown in Figure 2.1, the first type of transformation, maximize other's gain, represents pure altruism; a person who uses this transformation substitutes the other person's outcome for his or her own because the person values what the other person receives and will try to maximize that outcome. For example, a mother interacting with her baby might use such a transformation. With this transformation, it can be seen that the C-choice dominates the D-choice, and a person who makes such a transformation is likely to choose C. If both use this transformation, as shown in Figure 2.1, the result is likely to be the CC-outcome of (8, 8).

Secondly, for a person who uses a maximize-joint-gain transformation, the *sum of outcomes* for self and other is substituted for his or her own outcome, as shown in Figure 2.1. Again, the C-choice dominates the D-choice, and a person who uses this transformation is likely to choose C. If both use this transformation, the result is likely to be the CC-outcome for (8, 8). In contrast, a person who uses a maximize relative-gain transformation is motivated to gain more points than the other person, and substitutes *the difference* between the outcomes for self and other for his or her own. The resulting effective matrix, indicates that the D-choice dominates the C-choice, and the person is likely to choose D. If both use this transformation as shown in Figure 2.1, the result is likely to be the DD-outcome for (4, 4).

To enable predictions of choices in the PDG, it will be necessary to determine what type of transformation an individual is likely to make. Messick and McClintock's measurement of social

Maximize Other's Gains

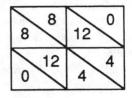

Given Matrix (PDG)

Maximize Sum

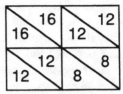

Maximize Difference

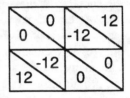

FIGURE 2.1
Example of Given Matrix (PDG) and three types of transformations resulting in three effective matrices. It is assumed that both players use the same transformation in each case.

values immediately comes to mind. An individual with a cooperative orientation should maximize the sum of outcomes, whereas an individual with a competitive orientation should maximize the difference in outcomes.

The Goal/Expectation Hypothesis

One of the most promising theories of cooperation in the PDG is Pruitt and Kimmel's (1977) goal/expectation (G/E) hypothesis. According to this hypothesis, the main reason that a person chooses C is to achieve the mutually cooperative CC-outcome. But if a person chooses C and the other person chooses D, the C-chooser will receive the CD-outcome, the "sucker's" payoff. Thus, the G/E hypothesis assumes that it is not sufficient to have the goal of achieving the CC-outcome: it is also necessary to expect that the other person will also choose C. In short, Pruitt and Kimmel state that two conditions must be satisfied for a person to choose C: (1) the individual must have the goal of achieving the CC-outcome, and (2) he/she must have the expectation that the other person will also choose C.

Pruitt (1983) describes several types of evidence to support the G/E hypothesis. For example, the fact that the tit-for-tat (TFT) strategy is most effective in inducing subjects to cooperate is consistent with their hypothesis. If a person chooses C with the goal of achieving the CC-outcome, TFT will reciprocate the C-choice, and will lead to the expectation that the other person is likely to choose C. Although not all subjects who interact with TFT recognize that the other person is using a reciprocal strategy. A recent study by Komorita, Hilty, and Parks (1991) showed that those who are aware cooperate more than those who are not aware.

Another important implication of the G/E hypothesis is that it is not restricted to the PDG and it can be generalized to other types of social situations. For example, Pruitt (1983) describes an extension of the hypothesis to a bargaining situation in which two bargainers must make concessions to reach a mutually profitable (cooperative) agreement. Efforts to reach a cooperative agreement may take many forms, such as, ". . . suggesting a possible compromise, providing information about the goals underlying one's demands so as to help the other locate a jointly acceptable alternative, signaling a willingness to make contingent concessions, participating in an informal problem-solving meeting with the other party, and cooperating with a mediator" (p. 112).

The extension of the G/E hypothesis to other social situations is important, but for the purpose of this book, the most important extension of the hypothesis is for the N-person social dilemma. This extension to the N-person case will be postponed to a later section of this chapter.

The Evolution of Cooperation

In one of the classic studies of the prisoner's dilemma game, Axelrod (1984) conducted a computer tournament to determine the effectiveness of various types of strategies (in maximizing own gain). Axelrod invited mathematicians and a variety of social scientists (economists, political scientists, sociologists, and psychologists) to submit a computer program to play the PDG in a round robin tournament. There were 14 entries and each program was pitted against each of the others for 200 trials. The tit-for-tat (TFT) strategy, submitted by Anatol Rapoport (a mathematician), was found to be most effective, as measured by the total score playing against all of the other entries. The TFT strategy begins with a cooperative choice on the first trial and then imitates the other person's choice thereafter. Thus, it is a reciprocal strategy, and as we shall see, reciprocity is a very important factor in facilitating cooperation in social dilemmas.

A second tournament was also conducted with a larger number of entries. Those who were invited to submit programs were informed of the results of the previous tournament and that TFT had won the tournament. TFT again won the tournament. The intriguing question is why TFT was so effective. Axelrod describes four important properties of TFT: (1) It is a "nice" strategy in that it is never the first to defect; (2) It cannot be exploited—it immediately retaliates if the other defects; (3) It is "forgiving" and immediately returns to cooperation if the other returns to cooperation after a defection; and (4) It is clear and easily understood. Axelrod suggests that one or more of these properties may be the underlying bases of TFT's effectiveness.

Axelrod then conducted a computer simulation in which various strategies were pitted against each other over 1000 separate tournaments (each with 200 trials). However, the entries in each tournament varied according to their success in the previous tournaments. Thus, Axelrod simulated an environment in which a strategy would be adopted ("survive") in succeeding tournaments ("generations") in direct proportion to its total score ("success") in previous generations. Over 1000 generations of the computer simulation, the remarkable result was that TFT was most successful in "reproducing" itself and replacing all of the other strategies. It is remarkable because it did not beat any of the other strategies in head-to-head contests. Since it is a "nice" strategy and is completely reciprocal, it does not exploit and cannot be exploited by other strategies. Its success could be attributed to the fact that the other "strong" (effective) strategies were very ineffective against each other; they were initially very effective in exploiting "weak" strategies, but when the weak strategies decreased in number and eventually became "extinct," the exploitive strategies also decreased in number because they destroyed the very environment that they needed to survive.

Based on these results Axelrod provides four suggestions on how to play the PDG.

1. *Don't be envious.* Don't compare your outcomes with the outcomes of the other person. Such comparisons may lead to temptation to defect, resulting in reciprocity of defection.
2. *Don't be the first to defect.* Defection is likely to lead to retaliation and an escalation of the conflict.
3. *Reciprocate both defection and cooperation.* TFT reciprocates defection (retaliates) immediately, and thus, it cannot be exploited. It also reciprocates cooperation immediately and thus facilitates mutual cooperation.
4. *Don't be too clever.* A clever (complex) strategy may be effective under certain conditions, but in general, it may lead to misperception and miscommunication of intentions, and may not lead to mutual cooperation. TFT is simple and predictable and communicates intentions clearly.

How to Promote Cooperation

Axelrod states that cooperation is very difficult to develop in the PDG if it is not played repeatedly.

> "That is why an important way to promote cooperation is to arrange that the same two individuals will meet each other again, be able to recognize each other from the past, and to recall how the other has behaved until now. This continuing interaction is what makes it possible for cooperation based on reciprocity to be stable."
> (1984, p. 125).

This statement is summarized by a proposal involving five ways to promote cooperation, in general:

1. *Enlarge the shadow of the future.* By this he means that the participants should anticipate future interactions with the same person. The greater the probability that the PDG will continue for many trials, the greater the expected reward for mutual cooperation. In the limiting case of a one-trial PDG, it is very risky and there is very little motivation to cooperate. In contrast, if the parties expect to interact for a large number of trials, they will be highly motivated to cooperate. These hypotheses have been supported by the results of a study by Murnighan and Roth (1983).

2. *Change the payoffs.* In terms of the payoff values of T, R, P, and S, we can make the reward (R) for mutual cooperation greater, or make the punishment (P) for mutual defection more severe.

3. *Teach people to care about each other.* Teaching altruism (unselfish caring for the welfare of others) is another way of promoting cooperation. A society of caring people are more likely to cooperate with each other than people who do not care about each other. However, Axelrod also states that there is a serious problem with altruism. A selfish person can exploit the generosity of altruistic members of society. Thus, such persons must be treated differently, and we should be altruistic to everyone initially, but thereafter only to those who show similar behavior. Axelrod then states, "But this quickly takes one back to reciprocity as the basis for cooperation" (p. 136).

4. *Teach reciprocity.* Tit-for-tat won both tournaments and it reciprocates both cooperation and defection. If we teach others to reciprocate, "You also have a private advantage from another person using reciprocity even if you never interact with that person: the other's reciprocity helps to police the entire community by punishing those who try to be exploitive. And this decreases the number of uncooperative individuals you will have to deal with in the future." (1984, p. 139).

5. *Improve recognition abilities.* To reciprocate the choices of others, it is necessary to recognize the other persons' behavior from past interactions. If people realize that a person who defects will remain anonymous, it will be difficult to punish those who defect. Since the temptation to exploit others through defection will be much greater if the exploiters cannot be identified, it is important that people can clearly recognize and identify those with whom they interact.

Some Restrictions

The results of Axelrod's computer simulation have extremely important implications for the evolution of cooperation, and for explanations of cooperation in a variety of settings—in business, in Congress, in warfare, and in biological systems. However, there are some important restrictions on the generality of his results and conclusions. First, Axelrod's findings are restricted to the two-person PDG, and may not generalize to other types of two-person games. His results are also restricted to a symmetric game in which the choices and pattern of outcomes are identical for the two parties, and in many social situations, outcomes are not always symmetric.

Secondly, Axelrod states that for cooperation to be stable, "the future must have a sufficiently large shadow. This means that the importance of the next encounter between the same two individuals must be great enough to make defection an unprofitable strategy when the other player is provocable. It requires that the players have a large enough chance of meeting again and that they do not discount the significance of their next meeting too greatly" (p. 174).

Thirdly, the success of a given strategy (such as TFT) is partly a function of the set of strategies it is pitted against, and its success depends on the environment in which it is placed. For example, Axelrod states that, "There is no ideal strategy independent of the strategies used by the others. In some extreme environments, even Tit-For-Tat would do poorly—as would be the case if there were not enough others who would ever reciprocate its initial cooperative choice. And Tit-For-Tat does have its strategic weaknesses as well (cf. Tetlock, McGuire, & Mitchell, 1991). For example, if the other player defects once, Tit-For-Tat will always respond with a defection, and then if the other person does the same in response, the result would be an unending echo of alternating defections" (p. 176).

The N-person Prisoner's Dilemma

In Chapter 1 we indicated that the prisoner's dilemma is one of several types of social dilemmas. The N-person prisoner's dilemma ($N \geq 3$) is simply an extension of the two-person case, and the constraints are very similar to those of the PDG. The essential conditions of the N-person case, hereafter denoted NPD, are as follows:

1. Each of the N-persons has two choices, cooperate (C) or defect (D);
2. The outcomes for each choice increase monotonically with the proportion of members who make the cooperative C-choice;

3. The D-choice yields a higher outcome than the C-choice no matter how many members choose C; and

4. The outcome if everyone chooses C is greater than the outcome if everyone chooses D.

Note that Condition 3 specifies that the D-choice dominates C, as in the PDG, and Condition 4 specifies that the outcome if all choose D is not Pareto optimal. Despite these similarities in the conditions of the two-person and the N-person cases, there are some important qualitative differences.

Dawes (1980) for example, claims that the PDG is unique and is not representative of social dilemmas in general. First, when a person defects in the two-person case, the harm (or cost) is directed completely at the other person. In larger groups, in contrast, the harm for defection is diffused over a large number of persons. Secondly, when a person defects in the N-person case, the defecting behavior is anonymous; in contrast, in the two-person case, there is no uncertainty about the identity of the defector. Finally, when the two-person PDG is iterated (repeated over trials), each person can "punish" the other person by defecting on the next trial, or "reward" the other by cooperating on the next trial. Thus, each person has complete control of reinforcement of the other person, and can attempt to shape the other person's behavior. In the N-person case, it is not possible (or is very difficult) for one person to shape the behavior of the others. Despite these important differences, we have described the two cases in the same chapter because many variables have been found to have similar effects in the two cases.

The outcomes in the NPD can be represented geometrically as a function of the proportion of members who choose C. For illustrative purposes, we shall restrict our example to the case of payoff functions that are linear with equal slope, as shown in Figure 2.2. The notations C_i and D_i represent the outcomes for the C- and D-choices, respectively, and the subscripts denote the number of persons who choose C. For example, the points C_1 and D_1 denote the outcomes for C- and D-choices, respectively, when one person chooses C. Similarly, the points C_{N-1} and D_{N-1} denote the outcomes for the C- and D-choices, respectively, when $N-1$ persons choose C. The point C_0 cannot occur since none choose C; similarly, the point D_N cannot occur since all members choose C.

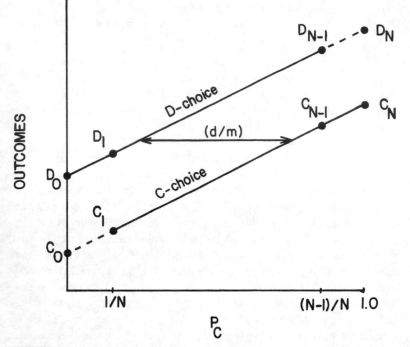

FIGURE 2.2

Geometric representation of N-person prisoners' dilemma game.
Note: (1) P_c denotes proportion of members who cooperate (choose C);
(2) D and C denote outcomes for defection and cooperation, respectively;
(3) subscripts denote the number of persons who choose C; and (4) d/m
denotes the horizontal distance between outcomes for the D and C-choices.

From S. S. Komorita, "A model of the N-person dilemma-type game." in *Journal of Experimental Social Psychology*, 1976, vol. 12, pp. 357–383. Copyright © 1976 Academic Press. Reprinted by permission.

An Index of Cooperation

Consider the 5-person game shown in Table 2.7. This is the same game as the game in Table 1.3 discussed in Chapter 1. The only difference between the games in Table 1.3 and Table 2.7 is that in Table 2.7 we depict the outcomes in terms of the *total number of persons who choose C*, whereas in Table 1.3, the outcomes are depicted in terms of the *number of others who choose*. We present the game in Table 2.7 so that the outcomes will correspond to the geometric representation in Figure 2.2. Nonetheless, the two games are identical. For this game, $D_0 = 2$, the outcome for the D-choice

TABLE 2.7 Five-person Prisoner's Dilemma

	Number of Persons Choosing C					
	0	1	2	3	4	5
D	2	4	6	8	10	—
C	—	0	2	4	6	8

when none choose C, and $C_1 = 0$, the outcome for the C-choice when one person chooses C. Similarly, $D_{N-1} = 10$, the outcome for the C-choice when 4 members $(N-1)$ choose C, and $C_N = 8$, the outcome for the C-choice when all choose C.

As an extension of Rapoport's K-index for the two-person PDG, Komorita (1976) proposed the following index for the N-person case:

$$K' = \frac{C_N - D_0}{D_{N-1} - C_1} \qquad (2.2)$$

Under the constraints of the NPD, the K' index varies from 0 to 1 $(0 < K' < 1)$, and for the game shown in Table 2.7, $K' = (8 - 2)/(10 - 0) = .60$. Like the K-index, the larger the value of K', the greater the level of cooperation that is predicted. Indeed, when $N = 2$ (PDG), note that $D_{N-1} = T$, $C_N = R$, $D_0 = P$. and $C_1 = S$, where T, R, P, and S are the general (symbolic) values of the two-person game that we described earlier [see Table 2.1b]. If we substitute these values in Equation 2, it can be seen that $K' = (R - P)/(T - S)$, which is the same as Rapoport's K index (see Equation 2.1).

With regard to the validity (accuracy) of K' in predicting levels of cooperation, Figure 2.3 shows data from three different studies with varying group sizes. Data for $N = 2$ are from Rapoport and Chammah (1965); data for $N = 14$ are from Kelley and Grzelak (1972), and data for $N = 3$ and $N = 4$ and 8 are from Komorita, Sweeney, and Kravitz (1980). The solid and open triangles, circles, and squares denote data from separate experiments. It can be seen that P_C, the mean proportion of cooperative (C) choices, increases directly with values of K'. In addition, note that P_C decreases with group size (N); P_C is greatest for $N = 2$ and lowest for $N = 14$. As we shall see, this inverse relation between P_C and group size is predicted by the K' index.

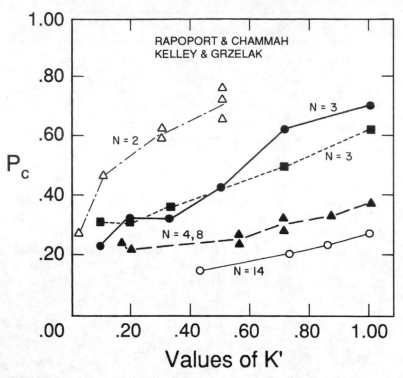

FIGURE 2.3
Proportion of cooperative choices (P$_C$) as a function of K′
From S. S. Komorita, James Sweeney, and David A. Kravitz, "Cooperative Choice in the N-person Dilemma Situation" in Journal of Personality and Social Psychology, 1980, Vol. 38, No.3, pp. 504–516. Copyright © 1980 American Psychological Association. Reprinted by permission of the publisher.

Another interesting factor, closely related to the K′ index, is the d/m parameter proposed by Schelling (1973). The d/m parameter represents the horizontal distance between the payoffs for the C- and D-choices as shown in Figure 2.2. When the slopes of the two payoff functions are equal (as in Figure 2.2), the horizontal distance between the two functions is equal to d divided by m, where d denotes the vertical distance between the two payoff functions, and m denotes the slope of the two functions. The d/m parameter is also an index, and under the constraints of the NPD, d/m varies from 0 to 1 (0 < d/m < 1). When d/m = 0, the payoffs for the C and D-choices are the same, and there would be no dilemma. Conversely, when d/m = 1, the payoff when all defect is the same as the payoff when all choose C, and there would be no incentive to choose C. It can be shown that there is a one-to-one (inverse) correspondence between the K' index and Schelling's d/m parameter: The larger K', the smaller the value of d/m (when $d/m = 0$, $K' = 1$, and when $d/m = 1$, $K' = 0$).

Note that the horizontal distance between the two functions represents a proportion of the N-members. In the context of a society of N-members, Schelling hypothesizes that a political action group (a coalition formed to influence the behavior of other members) is not likely to be effective unless it attracts a proportion of members at least as large as d/m. For example, in the situation depicted in Figure 2.2 d/m is approximately 50 percent of the members (one-half of 0 to 1.0), and according to Schelling's hypothesis, an effective action group must consist of at least 50 percent of the members.

Schelling's hypothesis is based on the following reasoning. Suppose all members of society pursue their selfish interest (defect), resulting in a payoff of D_O in Figure 2.2. If a coalition of size d/m can be formed, the members can switch (by concerted action) to the cooperative choice *without loss*. Indeed, if the coalition is larger than d/m, the members can actually increase their payoff by switching to the C-choice. In subsequent stages, the coalition will attempt to induce others to join the coalition, and if another subset of size d/m is added to the original coalition, the new members can switch to the C-choice without loss. Moreover, the coalition can threaten to revert to the D-choice if others refuse to join the coalition, and this threat is credible because they can return to the D-choice without loss.

Group Size and Cooperation

When the d/m parameter is held constant, the value of K' decreases with group size (N). This relation between K' and group size is shown is Figure 2.4. It can be seen that the decrease in K' occurs for small values of N (between 2 to about 20) and then there is negligible change thereafter. Since P_C, the mean proportion of members who cooperate, is directly related to the magnitude of K' (Figure 2.3), this means that cooperation should decrease with group size. Indeed, several investigators have hypothesized that cooperation in a group should decrease with group size (Hamburger, Guyer, & Fox, 1975; Marwell & Schmitt, 1972; Messick, 1973; Olson, 1965), and there are several empirical studies that support this hypothesis.

There are several explanations for this inverse relation between cooperation and group size. Marwell and Schmitt (1972) hypothesize that subjects in an N-person dilemma situation typically

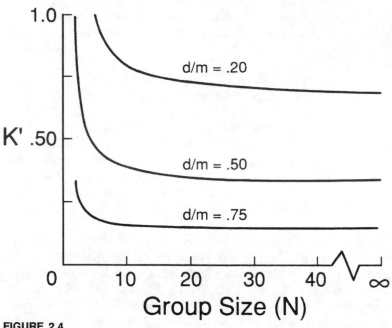

FIGURE 2.4
Values of K' as a function of group size.

From S. S. Komorita, "A model of the N-person dilemma-type game" in *Journal of Experimental Social Psychology,* 1976, vol. 12, pp. 357–383. Copyright © 1976 Academic Press. Reprinted by permission.

react to defection with defection, and if one person becomes exploitative, others are likely to reciprocate. Since the probability that at least one person in the group will defect (begin the exploitative cycle) increases with group size, cooperation should be less likely in larger groups. Olson (1965) and Messick (1973) propose a second explanation based on the relative effect of a person's choice on the final outcome. In a large group a person's choice has little effect on the outcome, but in a small group a person's choice has a much larger effect. Thus, if the group fails to achieve a given level of cooperation, there is a "diffusion of responsibility" for the failure, and both Olson and Messick predict that cooperation should decrease with increasing group size.

A third explanation, similar to the second, is based on the concept of "deindividuation." The concept of *deindividuation* refers to a state in which individuals act as if they are "submerged in the group," are not seen or paid attention to as individuals, and do not feel that they stand out as individuals (Festinger, Pepitone, & Newcomb, 1952, p. 382). Zimbardo (1970) hypothesizes that a crucial factor in deindividuation is anonymity, and showed that a state of deindividuation leads to antisocial behaviors. Under the assumption that deindividuation leads to an increase in uninhibited behaviors, Hamburger, Guyer, and Fox (1975) hypothesized that group size increases deindividuation, which in turn, increases the likelihood of the selfish defecting choice. This hypothesis is supported by the fact that one of the basic differences between the two-person and the N-person cases is that in the latter case, there is anonymity of choices. In the two-person case, when a person defects there is no uncertainty about the identity of the defector. In the N-person case, as in the five-person game of Table 2.7, if one person chooses D and all of the others choose C, the defector cannot be identified. Thus, there is complete anonymity of choices in the N-person case, which satisfies one of Zimbardo's (1970) basic criteria of deindividuation.

To the extent that deindividuation inhibits cooperative behavior, it is reasonable to assume that any procedure that reduces deindividuation should enhance cooperative behavior. Consequently, if each member of the group can be identified and his/her choice is made known, deindividuation may be eliminated or minimized. This opposing state in which group members are identified and singled out as individuals is called "*individuation*" (Zimbardo, 1970). The results of several studies support the hypothesis that individuation may enhance cooperative behavior in social dilemmas. In these studies, a higher level of cooperation was obtained when individual choices were disclosed publicly than when they were made anonymously (Bixenstine, Levitt, and Wilson, 1966; Fox and Guyer, 1978).

Deindividuation research argues that cooperative behavior can be enhanced by making people more self-aware. By contrast, research on *group identity* would suggest that cooperation is improved by making people *less* self-aware. Group identity refers to a person's affiliative ties to a group and the extent to which he/she identifies with the group. Brewer (1979, 1981) and Edney (1980) argue that the greater an individual's feelings of affiliation and identification with a group or community, the greater the pressure on that person to make cooperative choices for the common good. Kramer and Brewer (1984) demonstrated this empirically. In their study, subjects were made to feel as either part of a group (by being told that the responses of all subjects would be combined and compared to subjects from another school) or an isolated individual (by being told that each subject's behavior would be analyzed separately). Kramer and Brewer found that subjects who felt like a group member made many more cooperative choices than subjects who felt like an individual. In contrast, deindividuation research would make the opposite prediction: lumping subject responses together creates anonymity, and defectors cannot be detected, so we should see high rates of defection. It is not clear at this point how these inconsistent results can be explained.

Yamagishi's Structural Goal/Expectation Approach

For the N-person social dilemma, Yamagishi (1986b) has proposed a theory that is based on an extension of Pruitt and Kimmel's (1977) goal/expectation hypothesis (discussed earlier). Yamagishi hypothesizes that an individual's tendency to cooperate depends on *"action-interdependence,"* the belief that one's action will significantly influence the behavior of others in the group, and in particular, whether others will reciprocate one's cooperation. However, Yamagishi also claims that these beliefs may be reasonable in a dyad or in a very small group, but in a large group this expectation of action-interdependence may be difficult to develop because a single member's action "has very low visibility to other members. Thus, even those who have developed the goal of mutual cooperation will hesitate to cooperate because of the fear that their cooperation will be exploited" (p. 70).

Yamagishi implies that the goal/expectation hypothesis may not be applicable in large groups, and consequently, he proposes an extension called the "structural goal/expectation" theory. This theory assumes that some type of coercion is needed to facilitate cooperation, especially in large groups, and the reward structure of the social dilemma must be changed. For this purpose, members are given the opportunity to change the reward structure by introducing a sanctioning system that imposes a penalty for defection, a reward for cooperation, or both. If the costs of implementing the sanctioning system are lower than the gain for cooperation, the dilemma vanishes.

The problem is that the decision to implement the sanctioning system introduces another dilemma, called a second-order dilemma. Thus, two types of dilemmas are distinguished: the original dilemma and the second-order dilemma. Two types of cooperative acts are distinguished, corresponding to the two types of dilemmas: elementary and instrumental cooperation, respectively.

Yamagishi admits that it may be difficult in some cases to resolve the second-order dilemma because instrumental cooperation also requires the development of action-interdependence. Nonetheless, he argues that the conflict in the second-order dilemma is not as severe as in the original dilemma, for the following reasons: First, some social dilemmas (e.g., resource dilemmas) may involve severe conflict of interests among the members (a large majority of cooperators can be exploited by a few defectors). In contrast, in a second-order dilemma, the loss for the cooperators is limited to the small resources contributed to implement the sanctioning system. Secondly, assuming that most members are motivated to achieve mutual cooperation—as predicted by the goal/expectation hypothesis—instrumental cooperation should be enhanced because it is specifically designed to encourage everyone to cooperate in the original dilemma. Thus, Yamagishi claims that the obstacles to instrumental cooperation are much less critical in a second-order dilemma.

The results of several empirical studies directly support the effectiveness of sanctioning systems (Yamagishi and Sato, 1986; Yamagishi, 1986a). In particular, Yamagishi's theory predicts that subjects must experience the futility of achieving mutual cooperation through voluntary means, and must come to the realization that a structural change is necessary to achieve mutual cooperation. The results of several studies provide indirect support for this prediction, but because many of the tests of his theory are based on public goods and resource dilemmas, we shall postpone a description of these studies to subsequent chapters of this book.

Summary

A special case of a social dilemma is the prisoner's dilemma. In both the two-person PDG and the N-person case, each person has two choices: cooperate (choose C) or defect (choose D). Defection yields a higher outcome than cooperation, no matter what the other member(s) choose. Thus, it is individually rational for each member to defect. Yet, if all defect, all are worse off than if all cooperate. Thus, the axioms of individual and collective rationality are in conflict. Studies that varied the reward structure (payoff values of the outcome matrix) indicate that the results are consistent with reinforcement principles: The greater the reward for the cooperative choice and the greater the punishment for defection, the greater the mean proportion of cooperative choices.

Another important factor that affects cooperation is the expected behavior (strategy) of the other person. If the other person is cooperative and always cooperates, they are likely to be exploited with defection. Similarly, if the other person is very competitive and always defects, such behavior is likely to be reciprocated. The most effective method of inducing subjects to cooperate is to use a reciprocal tit-for-tat strategy that cooperates on the first trial and then imitates the subject's response on the previous trial.

Several theoretical developments concerning cooperation in the PDG were discussed: (1) the measurement of motivational orientation (or social values) first proposed by Messick and McClintock (1968); (2) Kelley and Stahelski's (1970a, 1970b) attributional approach; (3) Kelley and Thibaut's (1978) theory of interdependence; (4) Pruitt and Kimmel's (1977) goal/expectation hypothesis; and (5) Axelrod's (1984) computer simulations.

Finally, an extension of the PDG to the N-person case (N > 2) was discussed. The dilemma in the N-person case is similar (but not identical) to the dilemma in the two-person PDG. Several investigators have hypothesized that cooperation should decrease with increasing group size, and there is considerable evidence to support this hypothesis. Several explanations for this inverse relation between group size and cooperation were discussed. The most notable were explanations based on: (1) perceived impact—in a large group one person's choice has very little effect on the outcome, and (2) group identity and deindividuation—in a large group there is greater anonymity and less identification with the group.

Public Goods

What Are Public Goods?

Consider a public television station. While the station receives some money from the government, the bulk of its funding comes from private donations, and as such, viewer contribution is crucial to the station's continued existence. However, it would be almost impossible for the station to prevent a noncontributor from watching its programs. From the individual viewer's standpoint, the question becomes, "Should I send money to the station when my contribution is not necessary for me to enjoy its product?"

On the face of it, the smart thing to do is to not contribute. You enjoy the "good" (public television programs) without having to give up something (money) to obtain it. But suppose that most of the station's audience acts similarly. In fact, suppose that of all the people that watch the station's programming, only a few actually send in some financial contribution. As a result, total contributions would fall far short of what is needed to continue broadcasting, and the station would go off the air. Now no one, contributors and non-contributors alike, may enjoy their favorite public television programs, and everyone is worse off than they were before the fund drive began.

The situation confronting viewers of public television is an example of a *public goods* social dilemma. A public good is a product or service that can be "consumed" by members of a group, and its provision is almost entirely dependent on contributions by group members. A public good is distinguished from other types of consumer goods by two properties. First, the good has *jointness of supply*; it cannot be "used up" no matter how many group members consume it. Thus, your public television station will not "run out" of programming, even if everyone in the entire city tunes in at the exact same time. Second, a public good has *impossibility of exclusion*. This means that it is almost impossible to restrict noncontributors from consuming the good. Even if your public television station were able to find out that you were a noncontributing viewer, there is almost nothing they could do to restrict your regular consumption of their programs.

Recall that the defining characteristic of a social dilemma is the conflict between individual and collective rationality. The principles of jointness of supply and impossibility of exclusion make it clear what the individually rational choice concerning public goods is: since your consumption of the good will not affect the amounts that other members can consume (jointness of supply), and since you cannot be prohibited from consumption (impossibility of exclusion), the individually rational thing for you to do is to not contribute to the good's provision. This is illustrated in Table 3.1. Regardless of whether the station gets enough donations to continue

TABLE 3.1 Possible Outcomes from Public Television

		Did the Station Get Enough Money?	
		No	*Yes*
Did you Contribute?	Yes	– money	TV – money
	No	0	TV

broadcasting, your personal outcome is greater if you do not give any money. In Table 3.1, the term "–money" denotes the amount contributed, and the upper-left cell has an outcome of "–money" because it is very unlikely the station would send your money back if they went out of business.

The conflict between individual and collective rationality lies in the method by which the public good is provided. Since the good's provision is almost entirely dependent on individual contributions, and since the good is one which all group members can use, it is thus collectively rational to contribute. In fact, if the good is not provided, *all* members will be worse off than if the good were provided. This fact can be seen in Table 3.1. Assuming that the value to you of the programming is more than your contribution (a safe assumption, because you would not normally pay more for something than it is worth to you), the upper-right cell (TV – money) is greater than the lower-left cell (0). A public good, then, meets our definition of a social dilemma.

Types of Public Goods

For our purposes, we will consider two main types of public goods. A *discrete* or *step-level* public good is one that can only be provided in its entirety: It is not practical to provide a lesser amount of the good. Further, a certain minimum amount of money (or number of contributors) is needed to provide the good. An example of a discrete public good is a bridge. Let us assume that the state of Missouri wants to build a new bridge over the Mississippi River. The cost of the bridge will be covered by a one-year tax imposed on all gasoline purchases in Missouri. The bridge meets our definition of a public good: It is being provided by contributions from Missouri drivers (the tax), use of the bridge could not easily be limited to Missouri drivers, and a bridge cannot be "used up." (Note that there is also the opportunity to free ride, at least for St. Louis-area residents, by buying one's gas in Illinois.)

What happens, however, if the gas tax generates only enough money to cover half of the cost of the bridge? It is useless to build only half of a bridge; consequently, the bridge will probably not be built at all. For this reason, the bridge is a discrete public good. Most psychological experiments of public good dilemmas examine discrete goods.

By contrast, a second type of public good can be provided at any level, and the level of provision is determined by the rate or amount of contribution. These are known as *continuous* goods. A charity is an example of a continuous good. We usually contribute to a charity by giving varying amounts of money or time and effort. However, one can easily free ride on such contributions, simply because a charity rarely refuses to help any one. If you need the services of the Muscular Dystrophy Association, they will not check to see if you gave money during their yearly telethon before helping you. We can also logically assume that the value of the good is greater than the cost of contribution. In other words, the services offered by a charity are likely worth more to you than the money or time you contribute.

A charity is a continuous public good because it can be provided in some degree regardless of how many contributors there are. Even if just one person gives some money, the charity will be able to offer help they otherwise could not. As more people contribute, the range and degree of assistance becomes broader. It is not necessary for there to be a certain minimum number of contributors before the charity can function; as long as there is at least one contributor, the good can be provided at some level.

Bridges and charities are two real-world examples of public goods social dilemmas. There are many other such examples. Libraries have jointness of supply and impossibility of exclusion, and are largely dependent for their provision upon contribution of some type. In fact, the services provided by a demoncratic government can be viewed as a public good. The nature of our legal system, health care, and military defense are all affected by the voluntary contributions (votes) of the public. However, our governmental bodies serve all citizens, voters and nonvoters alike. Consider the fact that it is individually rational not to vote (Meehl, 1977; Riker & Ordeshook, 1968), but if everyone acts rationally, the country and all of its citizens would be worse off.

Because of their pervasiveness, public goods dilemmas are attractive research topics for economists, political scientists, and sociologists, as well as psychologists. Indeed, the issue of public goods provision has a much longer history in economics than psychology.

Early Research on Public Goods

Economists have been interested in public goods-related issues since at least the 1930s, but the systematic study of public goods really began in the mid to late 1950s with a set of writings by Samuelson (1954), Musgrave (1959), and Head (1962). These works resulted in the ''jointness of supply'' and ''impossibility of exclusion'' principles that define public goods. In 1965 Mancur Olson wrote an influential book about public goods called *The Logic of Collective Action*. In this book Olson introduced the concept of "free riding." Free riding occurs when a person does not contribute to the provision of the good because by not contributing, one is "riding for free" on the contributions of others. Olson argued that the temptation to free ride is so strong that public goods will almost never be provided, because almost nobody will contribute to their provision.

If this were strictly true, however, then things like the March of Dimes charitable organization or clean water would not exist. Clearly, some people in society do contribute to certain public goods. To account for this, Brubaker (1975) modified Olson's original argument into what Brubaker called the "weak free-rider hypothesis." This hypothesis states that people will contribute to a public good, but the number of contributors will usually be *suboptimal*. For step-level goods, this means that not enough people will contribute for the good to be provided; for continuous goods, the amount of the good provided will be less than some desired level.

The weak free-rider hypothesis would seem to account for the fact that public goods are sometimes provided in our society. However, this hypothesis does not suggest *why* individuals choose to be individually rather than collectively rational. Why would someone ever act in a manner other than with self-interest? Further, the weak free-rider hypothesis does not suggest *how* free riding can be minimized and the provision of public goods increased. These are questions of interest to many psychologists. We will now explore some answers to these questions in greater detail.

Why Do People Free Ride?

It has only been over the last decade or so that psychologists have studied public goods in a systematic manner, and one of the main questions they have asked is (as you might expect), "When do people act collectively rational?" More specifically, when will (and why do) individuals go against their own best interests to help the group as a whole? Many factors have been proposed as possible answers to this question. We will focus on three such factors: self-efficacy, group size, and the "sucker effect."

Self-Efficacy

Think back to our public television example at the beginning of this chapter. One of the reasons a person might give for not contributing is that one small contribution would hardly make a difference. The belief that you have about the effect of your actions on the eventual result is known as *self-efficacy* (Bandura, 1986). Self-efficacy has long been thought to be an important variable in public goods behavior (Messick, 1973; Olson, 1965), and feelings of self-efficacy have been shown to exert a strong influence on a person's tendency to free ride: When people have a low sense of self-efficacy, they are more likely to free ride than when their sense of self-efficacy is high.

Norbert Kerr and his research associates have studied the relationship between self-efficacy and free riding in great detail. Kerr and Bruun (1983) found that feelings of self-efficacy are affected by method of provision of the good. In their study, whether or not a group received the public good (money) was determined by the level of performance of a physical task (blowing air into a pulmonary testing device). For some of the groups, the criterion for receiving the good was the performance of their *worst* group member, or the person achieving the lowest pulmonary test score; for other groups, provision was determined by their *best* member, or highest test score. Each subject performed a pretest with the device—ostensibly to establish their ability. However, Kerr and Brunn, actually gave each subject false feedback. Some subjects were told that their "ability" was high—their pretest score was better than 75 percent of all other subjects. The rest of the subjects were told that they had done poorly—75 percent of all other subjects had performed better than they. These subjects had low "ability." Subjects then learned of the "abilities" of their fellow "group members" (in actuality, there were no groups), and completed a number of trials with the pulmonary device.

The results of Kerr and Bruun's study are shown in Table 3.2. They found that in the "worst member" condition, those group members who thought they had high ability had a low sense of self-efficacy. In other words, the high-ability members felt there was little they could do to affect the group's chances of receiving the good. Conversely, in the "best member" condition, those with

TABLE 3.2 Results of Kerr and Bruun (1983)

Subject's Belief	Success Depends on	
	Best member	Worst member
High ability	High efficacy	Low efficacy
Low ability	Low efficacy	High efficacy

perceived low ability felt low self-efficacy. Low self-efficacy consequently decreased subjects' "contribution" ("pumping") in both conditions.

Kerr (1989) also showed that self-efficacy is affected by group size (a hypothesis that had earlier been offered by Messick, 1973, and Olson, 1965). He found that people believe that their ability to affect the group's outcome decreases as group size increases. Moreover, people will maintain this belief even when their actual self-efficacy stays constant. Kerr demonstrated this in two studies. Subjects in both studies were led to believe that they were part of a group that had the chance to provide a public good. In one study, individuals thought they were part of either a 9-person or a 30-person "group;" in the other study, "group" sizes were 4 persons or 100 persons. In reality, the choices made by the other members of the "group" were already determined by Kerr.

Kerr wanted the subject's contribution to be as crucial in the 30-person groups as it was in the 9-person groups; to accomplish this, the probability that "others" would contribute was higher in the large groups than in the small groups. Drawing on simple probability theory, Kerr (and also Rapoport, 1985) showed that objective self-efficacy, or the probability that one can actually affect the group's outcome, can be easily calculated with the following formula:

$$\text{OSE} = \binom{N-1}{p-1} P(C)^{p-1} [1 - P(C)]^{N-p} \qquad (1)$$

where OSE=objective self-efficacy, N=group size, p=number of contributors necessary to provide the good, and P(C)=the probability that others will contribute. If all other variables are held constant, OSE will decrease as N increases. However, OSE can be held constant if P(C) is increased along with group size. Table 3.3 numerically demonstrates these relations.

By increasing P(C) accordingly, Kerr was able to give subjects in a 30-person group as much OSE as subjects in a 9-person group. According to this logic, subjects in the 30-person group who believed that the probability others would contribute was .23 should have felt just as much self-efficacy as those in the 9-person group who thought P(C) was equal to .076. However, Kerr found that this was not the case; those in the large groups still expressed lower self-efficacy than those in the small groups. Kerr argued that people maintain a general belief that they will have little effect on the outcome of the large group (which he called the *illusion of efficacy*), and that this belief persists even when there is evidence against it.

TABLE 3.3 Objective self-efficacy (OSE)

Case 1: OSE decreases as N increases

P(C)	p	N	OSE
0.29	3	4	0.09
0.29	3	5	0.08
0.29	3	6	0.07

Case 2: OSE remains constant if N and P(C) increase

P(C)	p	N	OSE
0.29	3	4	0.09
0.31	3	5	0.09
0.41	3	6	0.09

Criticalness

Related to the issue of self-efficacy is the notion of criticalness. How do people behave when their actions will absolutely determine whether the good is provided? Stroebe and Frey (1982) have shown that in theory a positive relation between criticalness and contribution should exist: The more critical one perceives oneself to be, the more likely one is to contribute. Van de Kragt, Orbell, and Dawes (1983) devised a simple experimental technique, known as the *minimal contributing set (MCS) paradigm,* to empirically test this question. In the MCS paradigm (or procedure), each group member receives an "endowment" of money. In order for the good to be provided, a certain (minimum) number of group members have to contribute, and hence lose their entire endowments. If a sufficient number of members contribute, all persons receive the public good (usually money); if not, no good is provided. The members are allowed to discuss the dilemma and designate specific contributors. After discussion, each person *privately* decides whether to contribute or not. Thus, members who were designated a contributor could actually not contribute and guarantee that they would receive at least some money and no one would know.

Table 3.4 shows the payoff table for the MCS used by van de Kragt *et al.* In their study, each member of a 7-person group received an endowment of $5. In order to receive a public good worth $10 per person, three members had to give up their endowments. Despite the temptation of a guaranteed payoff in this experiment (and in van de Kragt, Dawes, Orbell, Braver, & Wilson, 1986), the

TABLE 3.4 Payoff Table for a Sample MCS Game

	No. of Other Contributors						
Your choice	0	1	2	3	4	5	6
Contribute	0	0	10	10	10	10	10
Not contribute	5	5	5	15	15	15	15

researchers found very little free riding; over 96 percent of all their groups had at least the minimum number of necessary contributors. In virtually all of the groups, three persons were designated by the group to contribute their endowment of $5. For this reason, van de Kragt, *et al.* called these designated members, "the minimal contributing set." The important point is that these members were critical in providing the good ($10) to all group members. Rapoport, Bornstein, and Erev (1989) also found a strong relation between perceived criticalness and contribution, and Stroebe and Frey (1982) have provided a theoretical basis for the criticalness-contribution relation. The knowledge or belief that one's actions are critical to the group's success thus seems to have a strong influence on one's contribution behavior.

An important fact to understand about the MCS paradigm is that defection (not contributing) does not strictly dominate contributing. When one is "critical" (the group's success or failure is completely determined by one's actions), it is personally better to contribute. This is seen in Table 3.4 when the number of other contributors equals 2. A contribution results in a payoff of $10; however, withholding contribution will produce only $5. Despite the fact that defection does not dominate cooperation, the MCS paradigm meets the conditions of a social dilemma that we proposed in Chapter 1. Indeed, we have already encountered a dilemma game in which defection does not dominate cooperation. Recall the game of CHICKEN in Chapter 2. In CHICKEN defection does not dominate cooperation, but it meets the essential conditions of a social dilemma: If all members attempt to maximize selfish interests, all are worse off than if all attempt to maximize collective interests. The important point is that the nature of the dilemma in the MCS paradigm may be qualitatively different from the dilemma in other types of public good dilemmas in which defection dominates cooperation (contribution).

TABLE 3.5 Outcomes of A Volunteer's Dilemma

Your Choice	Number of Other Volunteers			
	0	1	2	3
Volunteer	Football car wear	Football car wear	Football car wear	Football car wear
Not volunteer	Nothing	Football	Football	Football

A special case of a minimal contributing set is the Volunteer's Dilemma (Diekmann, 1985, 1986). Consider the following example. A group of four students wants to go to a (nontelevised) football game. All have cars, but none want to subject their car to the wear and tear of a long freeway drive or take a chance that the car will be damaged in the crowded parking lot. However, if nobody drives, no one can see the game. One person must *volunteer* to receive a lesser outcome (football minus wear on the car) so that all others can receive the good (football).

The outcome matrix for this situation is shown in Table 3.5. You can see that not volunteering generally yields a higher payoff than volunteering, except when nobody else volunteers; in this instance, all are worse off than if at least one person had volunteered. With the Volunteer's Dilemma, the minimal contributing set is 1; in other words, the good will be provided if one person contributes.

Volunteer's Dilemma-type situations sometimes have tragic overtones. Consider the phenomenon of bystander intervention (Darley & Latane, 1968; Latane & Darley, 1970). A group of bystanders observe a person being attacked, and must decide whether to intervene. All would like to see someone volunteer to help the person, but all must consider the potential costs of volunteering (e.g., being physically harmed by the attacker). It is generally better not to help; if someone else does, then all can experience the satisfaction of seeing the attacker thwarted without having brought any danger upon themselves. However, if no one volunteers, then the victim will suffer and a tragedy will occur. As might be expected, research in bystander intervention indicates that the likelihood that people will help a potential victim is inversely related to the expected costs of helping, and directly related to the likelihood that the victim actually needs help. Moreover, as the number of bystanders increases, the likelihood that a particular bystander will help decreases, though the overall probability of help does not change (Latane & Nida, 1981).

Expectations

One reason group members might feel low self-efficacy has to do with expectations about others' behavior. Why should you contribute if you don't think anyone else will? Your contribution would just be wasted. One explanation offered by van de Kragt, Orbell, and Dawes (1983) for their findings is that each critical member expected the other critical members to do what they said they would (contribute). Indeed, expectations seem to be an important part of self-efficacy-based public goods behavior.

Amnon Rapoport and his colleagues have extensively studied the role of expectations in public goods. Rapoport (1985, 1987) and Rapoport and Bornstein (1987) have looked at how expectations are formed. In most public goods situations, it is very likely that you know almost nothing about your fellow group members. If you have almost no information about their personalities, values, or interests, how can you make predictions about their behavior? According to Rapoport, one method you might use is to make a *homogeneity assumption.* Here, you simply assume that all of the other group members have an equal probability of contributing to the public good. While this assumption is simple, in some situations it may be unrealistic. It is not unreasonable, for example, to assume that some people are more likely to give money to public television than others, even though you know very little about the entire group of public television viewers. Rapoport thus proposed a second method of forming expectations, the *heterogeneity assumption.* Under the heterogeneity assumption, you would select some probability values at random and assume that some people will contribute with each of those probabilities. For example, you might assume that some people are almost certain to contribute to public television (say, 95 percent), some people very unlikely (10 percent), and most people moderately likely (60 percent). Experimentally, Rapoport (1988) has found the heterogeneity assumption to be an accurate description of how expectations are initially formed.

Even in the most anonymous public good situations, however, you will usually possess at least some information about your fellow group members, and this basic information has been shown to have effects on your expectations about what others will do. For example, it is logical to assume that some group members have more *resources* (e.g., money, time) than others. Professors and poor students alike watch public television. Rapoport (1988) and Rapoport, Bornstein, and Erev (1989) have shown that your expectations can be based in part on these differences in resources. In their studies, individuals received a small, medium, or large endowment, that they could keep or contribute toward a public good. The researchers found that those with small endowments were perceived to be more likely to contribute than those with large endowments. Rapoport argued that this was because those with small endowments had less to lose if the good were not provided, and proportionately more to gain if it were provided, than those with large endowments.

Another piece of information that you have, of course, is your own behavior. Do your own preferences affect what you think others will do? Rapoport and Eshed-Levy (1989) suggest that they do. They showed that there is a generally strong positive relationship between whether or not you contribute and whether you think others will contribute (though as we will see a bit later, there is a situation where this does not occur). To put it simply, you will usually expect others to act as you do. This type of estimation strategy—to assume that others are like you—is actually not uncommon (Dawes, 1988). In fact, Orbell and Dawes (1991) have proposed a formal explanation of cooperation based on this strategy. In their theory, defectors expect others to defect as well; hence, defectors will not participate in the dilemma because they expect to end up in the "all-D" cell of the payoff matrix. By contrast, cooperators expect others to cooperate, and as a result, they choose to play the game. Since defectors are not participating, a cooperator will end up interacting with other cooperators and receive the large "all-C" payoff.

Group Size

We have seen that self-efficacy is an important factor in one's decision to contribute or not contribute to a public good. Clearly, you would like to feel that your contribution made a difference in the group's receiving the good. But how likely is it that you will be a critical member, or have any influence on the outcome, in a group as large as a television viewing audience? Would you be more likely to contribute if the group size were ten rather than in the hundreds? What role does group size play in contribution decisions?

We have already discussed some evidence on the effects of group size; recall that Kerr (1989) and Kerr and Bruun (1983) found that people generally believe they make less of a difference in larger groups. Kerr (1989) also found that large groups are generally perceived to be less effective at providing public goods than small groups. In Kerr and Bruun's (1983) study, they found that, for certain kinds of tasks, contribution levels (in terms of how high one's test score was), as well as perceived self-efficacy, declined as groups grew from two to four persons.

The results of these studies might make you wonder how public goods get provided at all. After all, real-world groups working toward a public good are almost always much larger than four persons. If people work less hard in a four-person group than in a two-person group, how can a group of hundreds get *anything* accomplished? The answer is that group size *by itself* does not seem to affect individual behavior, at least in social dilemma situations.

Many researchers (e.g., Isaac & Walker, 1988b; Marwell & Ames, 1979; Rapoport, Bornstein, & Erev, 1989; Stroebe & Frey, 1982) have shown that changing only group size has minimal effect on a person's public goods behavior. Individual contributions seem to be affected only when something else changes *along with* group size. For example, Isaac and Walker (1988b) showed that people will decrease their contributions to a good when increasing group size causes their enjoyment of the good to go down (e.g., a park becomes overcrowded). However, if enjoyment is not affected by group size, then people in large and small groups contribute at about equal rates. Another factor is criticalness. Rapoport (1988) has argued that one factor that changes with group size is the probability that a group member will be critical; as group size increases, the likelihood that any one member's contribution will be critical to the group's success declines. We have already seen that self-efficacy and criticalness can play a large part in people's decisions to contribute. If a particular group member will only contribute to a good if the contribution will "make a difference," then, it would be quite unlikely that the person would contribute if the group were large.

In the previous chapter, we learned that reciprocal strategies can affect individual choices in Prisoner's Dilemma-type situations. What role, if any, do they play in public goods situations? Komorita, Parks, and Hulbert (1992) examined how individual contribution decisions are affected by reciprocal strategies in groups of various sizes (three, five, or nine persons). They found that reciprocity did affect cooperative behavior: the rate of contribution increased as more and more group members used reciprocal strategies. However, this effect was attenuated by group size; overall contribution tended to decrease as group size increased. Komorita and colleagues explained this by suggesting that, as group size increases, it becomes harder to figure out the strategy of any one group member. If each person is using a different strategy, it will be very difficult to pick out the pattern of choices of a particular group member. Because of this "noise" caused by conflicting strategies, reciprocating the actions of a specific person may be ineffective in very large groups.

Anonymity

One factor that almost always increases with group size is anonymity. The larger the group is, the more you are able to "hide in the crowd;" in other words, your actions become less noticeable (Kerr & Bruun, 1981). If your actions are hard to detect, that means that you can free ride and very few others (if any) will know. In fact, Olson (1965) suggested that anonymity was a major factor in free riding. Kerr (1983) and Stroebe and Frey (1982) have also argued that anonymity is an important part of the decision to not contribute.

Taking advantage of anonymity to decrease one's effort is known as *social loafing* (Latane, Williams, & Harkins, 1979). Free riders can be thought of as social loafers. They are not expending "effort" (contribution) to help produce the group "product" (public good). What can be done to minimize social loafing? There is an extensive body of research that addresses this question. Many techniques have been suggested for reducing social loafing: increasing the identifiability of individual behavior (Kerr & Bruun, 1981; Williams, Harkins, & Latane, 1981), providing a standard of comparison to evaluate effort (e.g., Harkins & Szymanski, 1989), and providing an extra incentive for a strong effort (Shepperd & Wright, 1989), to name a few. To date, researchers have not yet tested whether these solutions will also work in a public goods situation. Such work may provide additional insights into how to increase individual contributions.

The Sucker Effect

Let's return for the moment to a person's decision not to give any money to our public television station. One issue that might enter into the decision is whether we want other noncontributors to benefit at our expense. This aversion to "carrying" free riders is known as the sucker effect (Kerr, 1983; Orbell & Dawes, 1981), and it has been proposed as another explanation for noncontribution.

Kerr (1983) suggested several possible reasons to explain the aversion to being a sucker. One reason is that being a sucker may violate some social norms, like equity (the greater your contribution, the greater your reward should be), social responsibility (everyone should give something to their group), and reciprocity. Potential contributors may also assume that others are free riding because the good is neither interesting nor worthy of provision, and one does not want to be seen as having helped provide a "useless" good. Kerr conducted a study to test these various propositions. He used a task now familiar to you, namely, the pumping of air into a pulmonary testing apparatus. Individuals in his study believed they were working with another person to provide a public good, but in actuality their "partner's" performance was predetermined by Kerr.

To test his hypotheses, Kerr created four different conditions. (1) In the Able-Fail condition, subjects thought their partner was capable of performing the test, but failed it; (2) In the Unable-Fail condition, subjects thought their partner was incapable of performing the test and failed; (3) In the Individual Model (IM) condition, subjects had no partner, but worked by themselves (independently) in the presence of another, capable "subject" who failed the test; (4) In a fourth (Control) condition, subjects worked alone. If the "equity" and "social responsibility" explanations are accurate, then subjects in the Able-Fail and Unable-Fail Conditions should perform much worse than subjects in the Control condition because their "partner" is not contributing to the group. If the "uninteresting good" explanation is accurate, subjects in Individual Model should perform worse than subjects in the Control condition, because subjects would see that another capable individual is not working hard and would assume that the good is not worth providing.

Kerr's pattern of results are shown in Table 3.6. For each condition, Kerr determined the proportion of subjects that successfully completed the pulmonary test. He found that subjects in both the Unable-Fail and Individual Model conditions performed *at least as well* as those in condition Control. (The mean for Unable-Fail is

TABLE 3.6 Results from Kerr's (1983) Study

| | Experimental Conditions | | | |
	Able-Fail	Unable-Fail	Individual Model	Control
Success Rate (%)	75.4	84.4	95.4	88.9

less than Control, but not significantly less.) Only those in condition Able-Fail performed worse than subjects in Control. Subjects avoided playing the sucker only when they thought their partner was not working as hard as he/she could. Kerr thus suggested that people will support others only if they believe others will not *exploit* their contributions; people would rather see a good go unprovided than be taken advantage of.

Kerr's study showed that when a partner is unable to perform a task, people are willing to play the sucker. Kerr and MacCoun (1985) documented another situation in which individuals may be more willing to "carry" (tolerate the free riding of) another person, namely, when one's partner is female. Traditional sex roles dictate that men should make greater contributions to a group than women (Unger, 1979). Because women are not "expected" to contribute much (by both other women and men), Kerr and MacCoun predicted that subjects of both sexes would carry a free-riding partner who was female. Conversely, neither sex would tolerate a male free rider, since males "should" do the bulk of the work in a group. Their predictions were confirmed in a study very similar to Kerr (1983). When the "partner" was female, subjects of both sexes worked harder at the pulmonary (pumping) test than when the partner was male. It could be argued that females were less physically able to perform the test, and so subjects worked harder to compensate for this. Kerr and MacCoun did in fact find a sex difference on ability, but it did not seem to mediate the observed performance effect.

Other Variables

Self-efficacy, group size, and the sucker effect all seem to be important factors in one's decision to contribute to a public good. It is unlikely, though, that they are the only three variables that a person takes into account when deciding whether or not to free ride. Indeed, researchers have begun studying many other variables that may play a part in one's contribution decision. We will summarize some of this research here.

Endowment Size
If you were to contribute your $20 to the public television station, and the station were to cease broadcasting, you would lose your money. If your income was $1000 a week, a loss of $20 would be

negligible. But what if you only made $100 a week? Then a loss of $20 (with nothing to show for it) is somewhat serious. What will you do when you have a lot (or little) at stake?

Rapoport (1988; Rapoport, Bornstein, & Erev, 1989) has investigated this question. He predicted that individuals with large endowments would be less likely to contribute than those with small endowments because they had more to lose if the good were not provided. (Recall from our discussion of self-efficacy that this is exactly what subjects said they expected would happen.) In one study, (Rapoport, Bornstein, & Erev), this in fact did happen: the lower a person's endowment was, the more often he/she contributed. However, Rapoport (1988) found exactly the opposite; those with large endowments contributed most often. It is unclear why this discrepancy occurred.

Kerr (1992) examined endowment size in relation to self-efficacy. In his study, subjects were told they were a member of a five-person group trying to provide a public good. Each member had an endowment of points that could be contributed in an all/nothing fashion. If total contributions exceeded 50 points, the good would be provided. The subject knew only the amount of his/her endowment. This amount varied from 1 to 50 points. Kerr was interested not only in how endowment size affected contributions, but also whether it affected feelings of self-efficacy. He found that both likelihood of contribution and feelings of self-efficacy increased with endowment size. At the extremes, a person with 1 point contributed only 7 percent of the time; those with 50 points contributed 92 percent of the time. This pattern is consistent with Rapoport (1988); taken together, they suggest that the relationship between endowment size and contribution is positive.

Vested Interests

In a typical public goods experiment, every member receives the same payoff from the good. In other words, if the good is provided, all members receive the same amount of the good. However, in the real world this is rarely the case. Some people will watch only a couple hours of public television, others quite a lot. The latter viewers have more to lose if the station ceases broadcasting, and thus have a higher *vested interest* in seeing that the good is provided. Does such vested interest affect contribution behavior? Isaac, McCue, and Plott (1985) found that it does. Subjects who received a large payoff from a good contributed much more on the average than subjects who stood to receive a small payoff.

Incentives

A common criticism of psychological research on public goods (and many other topics) is that subjects in the experiments are not given a large enough incentive to behave in some predicted manner. [Payoffs in some of the previously-discussed studies were maximums of $2.25 (Kerr, 1983), $5.00 (Komorita, Parks, & Hulbert, 1992), $9.80 (Rapoport & Eshed-Levy, 1989), and $15.00 (van de Kragt, Orbell, & Dawes, 1983).] In the real world our "payoffs" from public goods tend to be valued much higher. Perhaps people would contribute more if there were stronger incentives to do so.

The role of incentives in psychological processes comprises a separate topic of study which has produced much research. We examined some of this research in Chapter 2, and saw that while the results are inconsistent, the majority of studies show no effects of incentives. The findings on incentives and public goods are no exception. For example, Komorita, Parks, and Hulbert (1992) gave subjects either a $5.00 incentive or no incentive at all, and found no difference in contributions between the two conditions. By contrast, Kim and Walker (1984) obtained significant amounts of free riding (compared to a "small incentive" condition) by making the payoff for such behavior a maximum of $25.00. (Note, though, that Kim and Walker's entire sample size consisted of only five subjects. It is difficult to make generalizations about behavior based on observations of only five individuals.) It is not at all clear, then, how incentives figure into a person's contribution decision.

Strategic Behavior

Finally, it is possible that some people will contribute in order to deceive others into believing that he/she is cooperative. By doing so, the person can then free ride after everyone else has been induced to contribute. Andreoni (1988) investigated this question: do group members use contributions strategically? In other words, do people contribute not because they are concerned for the group's welfare, but because it can set others up to be double-crossed? His results suggest that they do not. However, his study design was quite different from those usually used by public goods researchers. For example, his subjects knew exactly how many times they were to play the game; in the typical study, subjects do not have this information. His findings would thus need to be replicated using a more standard research design before we can be reasonably confident about them.

How Can Free Riding Be Minimized?

We have looked at a number of possible explanations for why people will act in their own, rather than the collective's, best interests. We have also seen that society is heavily dependent on public goods for its continued existence. Given this, our second research question asks what, if anything, can be done to minimize free riding and encourage people to work for the group. One obvious method is to alter the voluntary nature of the dilemma and compel people to contribute. Governments often use this technique; for example, there are stiff penalties for cheating on one's income tax. However, this solution is often difficult to implement, as well as being impractical, for private institutions. For example, there is almost nothing your public television station could do to force you to contribute. For this reason, researchers look for remedies that are practical and easily implemented in real-world situations.

Effects of Discussion

Recall that van de Kragt and his colleagues (1983, 1986) found that groups that were allowed to talk about the dilemma provided the public good over 95 percent of the time. It is well-known that communication has positive effects on social dilemma behavior (Brechner, 1977; Dawes, MacTavish, & Shaklee, 1977; Edney & Harper, 1978; Jerdee & Rosen, 1974; Jorgenson & Papciak, 1981). We saw that one possible explanation for this abnormally high rate involved individual expectations about others' behavior. However, it is plausible that the very act of *discussing* the dilemma may somehow increase cooperative intent. Indeed, van de Kragt *et al.* (1986) suggested it was very likely that discussion was playing a significant role in their high provision rates. In fact, a number of studies have shown that allowing pre-decision interaction among group members substantially increases contribution rate (e.g., Braver & Wilson, 1986; Isaac & Walker, 1988a; Liebrand, 1984).

Communication, then, seems to be an effective method of enhancing cooperation, at least in public goods situations. Further, it is a "naturally occurring" technique in that people very frequently discuss public goods-type issues (e.g., political candidates, favorite programs on public television), and is thus both practical and easily implemented. The obvious question to ask is "*Why* is discussion so effective?" Researchers have differing viewpoints on the answer to this question. Some more traditional positions explain discussion's effectiveness via conformity, trust, and/or values (Messick & Brewer, 1983), variables that undoubtedly play some role in the process.

Orbell, van de Kragt, and Dawes (1988) tested several possible explanations. One explanation is that discussion triggers a general "norm of cooperation" within the group. This explanation holds that all individuals believe cooperative behavior is a "good" course of action, and the discussion makes this norm salient (see also Kerr, 1992). Orbell *et al.* found no support for this explanation. Two other explanations received some support from their data. (It is also possible that these two explanations interact.) One is that discussion can (but will not always) promote *group identity,* or a substitution of group regard for individual concern (Messick & Brewer, 1983). The second is that discussion allows members to make explicit promises as to how they will behave, and such promises can act as a binding "contract." However, the contract can only be made if *all* members make a promise; without unanimity, the pact will fold. In fact, Orbell and colleagues observed that subjects who failed to make a promise, when all others had done so, were strongly pressured by the group to make one. This last result is consistent with an earlier set of findings by Bonacich (1972, 1976) in which, during free discussion after a series of choices, cooperators exerted social pressure on defectors (in the form of name-calling and general condemnation) to alter their choice patterns on subsequent rounds.

A somewhat similar explanation for the effects of discussion has been offered by Bornstein and Rapoport (1988). Drawing on the notion of criticalness that we discussed earlier, Bornstein and Rapoport argue that discussion allows the group to coordinate their behaviors and emphasize to each other the extreme importance of each complying with the group's plan. This line of reasoning is similar to Orbell and colleagues' idea of a contract, but does not involve explicit promise making.

No Fear, No Greed

Earlier in this chapter, we discussed Kerr's (1983) "sucker effect" as an explanation for free riding: group members free ride because they fear being taken advantage of. Another way to conceive of fear in public goods is the fear that one's efforts will go to waste. If we are the only ones who contribute, and we cannot meet the critical level of contribution by ourselves, then our efforts have been for naught. The converse of the sucker effect is greed. Free riding occurs because people want to "have their cake and eat it too;" that is, group members desire the good *as well as* their contribution (the lower right cell of Table 3.1). Theoretically, if we could guarantee that individuals could not be played for a sucker and remove the element of greed, contribution rates should greatly improve.

The effects of fear and greed, and more importantly (for our purposes) their removal, have been investigated by a number of researchers. Most of these studies have used the No Fear (NF) and No Greed (NG) paradigms, developed simultaneously by Dawes, Orbell, Simmons, and van de Kragt (1986) and Rapoport (1987). The games are simple variants of the Minimal Contributing Set (MCS) paradigm that we discussed earlier, except that no discussion is allowed. The NF game works by employing a "money back guarantee:" Subjects are informed that if the good is not provided, contributors will get their contribution back. Similarly, the NG game enforces a "fair share" rule: Subjects are told that if the good is provided, noncontributors must give up their endowments. (Note that NG is not the same thing as coercion, because each member may freely choose at the outset whether to contribute.) Finally, it is also possible to combine both rules into a NF+NG game, although such a game would not be a social dilemma because contributing would always produce at least as good an outcome as not contributing.

Illustrations of each type of game, along with those for a typical MCS, are shown in Table 3.7. We will use e to indicate the value of the endowment, r the value of the public good, and m the number of contributors needed to provide the good. Further, we will assume that the public good has a greater value than the endowment; in other words, $r > e$. The upper part of the table (denoted MCS) is a generalized version of the van de Kragt *et al.* (1983) matrix that we examined in Table 3.4. Recall that not contributing is the individually rational choice to make, *except* when you can completely determine the group's fate (in other words, $m - 1$ others have contributed). With the No Fear (NF) matrix, note that all persons receive a payoff of e units when the good is not provided. However, if at least m people contribute, noncontributors receive a greater payoff ($e + r$) than contributors (e). Conversely, nonprovision of the good under the No Greed (NG) matrix gives noncontributors a higher payoff (e) than contributors (0), but all receive an equal payoff (r) if the good is provided. Finally, when NF and NG are combined, the contributor's payoff is always at least as good as the noncontributor's payoff.

TABLE 3.7 Outcome Matrix for MCS, No Fear (NF), No Greed (NG), and Combined (NF+NG) Games

	Number of Other Contributors					
	0	. . .	m − 2	m − 1	m	. . .	N − 1
MCS						
Contribute	0		0	r	r		r
Not contribute	e		e	e	e + r		e + r
NF						
Contribute	e		e	r	r		r
Not contribute	e		e	e	e + r		e + r
NG						
Contribute	0		0	r	r		r
Not contribute	e		e	e	r		r
NF + NG						
Contribute	e		e	r	r		r
Not contribute	e		e	e	r		r

Source: Dawes *et al.* (1986) and Rapoport and Eshed-Levy (1989)

Dawes *et al.* (1986) and Rapoport and Eshed-Levy (1989) have used the NF and NG games to examine the relative roles of fear and greed. Dawes and colleagues did a series of single-trial experiments in which each of seven group members received a $5 dollar endowment ($e = 5$) that could be contributed toward the provision of a $10/member public good ($r = 10$). In one study, at least three group members had to contribute in order for the good to be provided ($m = 3$); in the other studies, five contributors were necessary. Rapoport and Eshed-Levy assembled five-person groups to play the game over 25 trials. On every trial, each group member had $e = \$1.40$, the public good was $r = \$7$, and at least three people had to contribute ($m = 3$) for the good to be provided. Rapoport and Eshed-Levy also used Israeli, rather than American, subjects. In the NF condition of both studies, if the total number of contributors was less than three, contributors received a payoff equal to e rather than nothing at all; in the NG conditions, if the number of contributors was three or more, each noncontributor received r rather than $e + r$.

As you can see in Table 3.8, in both studies the NG condition evoked higher levels of cooperation, and these results suggest

TABLE 3.8 Mean contribution Rates in Dawes *et al.* and Rapoport and Eshed-Levy Studies

	Average Contribution Rate		
Study	MCS	NF	NG
Dawes *et al.*	47%	56%	83%
Rapoport & Eshed-Levy	37%	53%	63%

that greed is the stronger instigator of free riding. However, the results of the two studies differ as to the role of fear. Dawes and colleagues observed significant increases in contribution when NG was used, but removing the fear element did nothing to improve contribution. Poppe and Utens (1986) found the same pattern using a different, though MCS-based, single-trial paradigm.) By contrast, Rapoport and Eshed-Levy found that fear as well as greed played a significant role in noncooperative behavior, though greed was still the major motive. Finally, the results of a study by Komorita, Sweeney, and Kravitz (1980), using N-person iterated games, suggest that greed is more important than fear in inhibiting cooperation.

Before proclaiming these contradictory findings, it is important to recognize that methodological differences exist between the studies that may plausibly have produced the discrepancy. In particular, the studies were conducted in different cultures (America and Israel respectively). It is known that cultural differences can produce divergent patterns of behavior in social dilemmas. Yamagishi (1988a, 1988c) has systematically compared American and Japanese behavior in a public goods setting and found that Americans are generally more trusting and cooperative than Japanese, and that Japanese are more willing to cease membership in a group of free riders than are Americans. A similar rigorous comparison of Americans and Israelis has not yet been conducted, but it is entirely plausible that cultural differences exist that could explain the discrepancy between the Dawes et al. and Rapoport and Eshed-Levy studies.

In a similar vein, Yamagishi and Sato (1986) have argued that the relative importance of fear and greed is dependent on whether a good's provision is determined by the performance of the group's best or worst member. When provision is dependent on the best member (e.g., the quality of a school system that is paid for through property taxes will be heavily dependent on the largest landowner in the district), many people will realize that they themselves are not the group's best; as a result, these people should see no reason to exert effort (contribute). This is greedy behavior. Conversely, if the provision is determined by the worst member's actions (e.g., the ability to consume previously polluted water is totally dependent on the sewage treatment efforts of the "cheapest" polluter), it is possible that the person's performance will not be good enough to provide the good. All other contributions would thus be wasted. Group members that reason this way should thus withhold contribution out of fear. Kerr and Bruun (1983) had earlier presented data that hinted at the effects on contribution of these different provisional demands, and Yamagishi and Sato found direct evidence that supported their hypotheses.

Sanctions

While seemingly effective, Yamagishi (1986a, 1986b) has argued that each of the above two solutions (reducing greed and fear) has a flaw that may make it relatively weak in real, large groups. Using No Greed as a real-world solution to free riding could be functionally difficult. A public goods provider would have to identify all free riders and enforce a fair-share contribution. For example, your public television station would have to determine that you were free riding, and then make you contribute something. This process, while possible, would be extremely inefficient. The effectiveness of discussion depends, according to Yamagishi and Sato, on *trust* among the group members. In order for either promise making or coordination of behaviors to work, one must trust the other group members to act consistently with their promise or assigned behavior. This notion is drawn from Pruitt and Kimmel's (1977) goal/expectation theory that we discussed in the previous chapter: In order for cooperation to develop in the PDG, both members must believe (trust) that the other person will not exploit their cooperative choice. However, Yamagishi argues that in large groups, complete trust is very difficult to achieve. Because larger groups offer greater anonymity, the opportunity to double-cross and be unnoticed increases. For this reason, Yamagishi argues that it is very risky to be completely trusting in large groups. (Some support for this position can be found in Fox & Guyer, 1977.)

Given this, Yamagishi suggests that cooperation can be maximized in larger groups by means of a *sanctioning system*. Such a system consists of some form of punishment that has been voluntarily provided by all group members. The punishment could be either tangible (e.g., restricted access to the good) or intangible (e.g., social stigmatization). For example, your friends that watch public television and make contributions to its provision might chastise and embarrass you for not giving money to the station. To avoid such punishment, free riders will alter their behavior and begin to cooperate. Yamagishi (1986a) found that such a system was very effective in inducing others to cooperate, especially when the group members had little trust in each other. (Hardin, 1977, and Stroebe & Frey, 1982, have also suggested sanctions as an effective means of controlling free riding.)

Method of Contribution

Most psychological studies of public goods have used *discrete contributions*; that is, subjects must contribute either all of their endowment or nothing at all. But real-world contributions are usually *continuous;* one can give any amount one wishes. Just as you are not asked to contribute "all or nothing" to a public good, neither is every group member expected to give at exactly the same time. Indeed, goods providers often make use of past contributions to try and convince others to contribute. Yet most psychological experiments require all subjects to make their contribution decision at exactly the same time. As a result, some researchers have hypothesized that the constraints of discrete and simultaneous contribution themselves may inhibit cooperative behavior. Suleiman and Rapoport (1992) compared discrete and continuous contribution and found contribution rates to be greater when it was continuous (66 percent) rather than all-or-none (42 percent).

Regarding sequential versus simultaneous contribution, Erev and Rapoport (1990) showed that allowing individuals to make sequential choices evoked greater rates of contribution. When choice was simultaneous, only 14 percent of their groups had enough contributors to provide the good; by contrast, 67 percent of the sequential-choice groups were able to provide the good. Further, information about how many previous noncontributors there were was more important than the number of previous contributors. Erev and Rapoport proposed an "irrevocable binding" hypothesis to explain their results. The actions of early choosers dictate what later choosers do. For example, if the first two members of my five-person group do not contribute, and our minimal contributing set is 3, I *must* contribute if I want the good; I do not have the option of free riding. The nature of the contribution mechanism thus seems to have some effect on whether the public good is provided. (Harrison & Hirshleifer (1989) have also commented on this issue.)

Auction

Smith (1979, 1980) has addressed the issue of discrete versus continuous contribution by studying the effectiveness of *auction-based* methods of providing public goods. In essence, an auction method allows individuals to state how much of the public good they would like to use as well as how much they are willing to contribute toward its provision. These two pieces of information are then combined and it is determined if the group is willing to contribute enough to provide the desired amount of the good. If not, individuals are asked to rethink and restate their preferences and the calculations are redone. This process continues until the good is provided, or group members become unwilling to change their preferences any more, at which point the good is not provided.

The process of combination is highly mathematical; however, a verbal example of the process might be useful. Consider a four-person group. Assume that each member has an endowment of $50, any amount of which can be contributed toward the provision of a public good. For simplicity's sake, let us define the good as consisting of a continuous amount of "units" that have some value to the group members. We need to make two assumptions about the good: no one member can consume the entire good all by him/herself, and there are more than enough units to satisfy the demands of all group members. These assumptions are highly realistic. For example, no one person could use an entire park, and the typical park has space enough to accommodate many people.

We must first ask each group member how many units of the good he/she would like to receive. Let us assume that the four requests are for 42, 54, 17, and 91 units, for a total request of 204 units. Next, we ask each person how much he/she is willing to contribute (or "bid") toward the provision of the good. (Note that no member knows the requests of the others, nor the total request.) Assume that the four offers are $15, $17, $4, and $20, for a total bid of $56. The experimenter will have predetermined a dollars/unit function that indicates how much one unit of the good costs. These functions tend to be complex; for our purposes, let us set the function at $1 for 3 units. Applying this function, you can see that the total bid of 56 dollars would purchase 168 units of the good. This is less than the total request of 204 units, which would have required a total bid of $68; group members have thus underbid for the good, and it is not provided. The group members are told that they have not offered enough to pay for their total request, and that they must submit new requests and/or bids. We would continue this process until subjects bid enough to pay for the total request, or a set number of trials have been exhausted, at which point the good is not provided.

Smith (an economist) compared (1979, 1980) the Auction method to what he termed the "Free-Rider" method, in which subjects must unanimously agree to pay the cost of the requested good, or else it is not provided. The Free-Rider method is a variant of the discrete method used in the typical psychology study. In Smith's study, no communication was allowed, and subjects in six-person groups attempted to provide a monetary public good. The subjects received endowments of from five to ten units, which could be contributed in any amount. Smith found the auction method to be consistently better at providing goods than the Free-Rider method. The auction method has not yet been tested under systematic procedures, and it is not clear whether any psychological variables, like those described earlier, affect its usefulness. Nonetheless, the auction method may be another general solution to free riding.

Group Competition for Public Goods

A new line of research into public goods behavior addresses how individuals behave when they belong to a group that is competing with another group for a good. This research has been conducted by Amnon Rapoport and his colleagues. Rapoport and Bornstein (1987) devised an extension of the MCS paradigm, called an *intergroup public goods* (IPG) game, to study group competition. In the IPG, each group member receives an endowment that can be kept or contributed to the provision of the good. The group that has the greater total contribution receives the good. If both groups have the same amount of contribution, each group receives an equal portion of the good (typically, although not necessarily, one-half).

An obvious question to ask regarding group competition involves group size. On the face of it, it would seem that, if one group were larger than the other, the larger group would more often receive the good, simply because it contains more potential contributors. To test this, Rapoport, Bornstein, and Erev (1989) pitted a three-person group against a five-person group. (Total endowment was kept constant by giving each member of the three-person group a 5-unit endowment, and each member of the five-person group a 3-unit endowment.) Surprisingly, the large group did not dominate the small group; the good went to the large group 60 percent of the time, and to the small group 40 percent of the time (there were no ties). Further, the mean proportion of contributors in both groups was almost exactly the same (56 percent and 57 percent for large and small, respectively). Rapoport and Bornstein (1989) likewise found little difference in the provision rates of three- versus five-person groups. In our earlier discussion of group size, we drew the conclusion that size by itself has little effect on contribution behavior. These results are certainly consistent with that conclusion.

A second variable that has been proposed to affect group competition for a public good is communication. In the original IPG, group members are not allowed to discuss the competition with anyone else. Recall our discussion of communication earlier in this chapter. One finding we noted is that preplay discussion substantially increases contribution rate when one group is striving to receive a good. But how effective is communication when that group is competing with another for the good? Two studies (Bornstein & Rapoport, 1988; Rapoport & Bornstein, 1989) showed that, consistent with previous research, preplay discussion within each group substantially improved contribution rates. In the 1988 study, contribution increased from 46 percent to 83 percent; in the 1989 study, it went from 47 percent to 82 percent. In addition, Bornstein, Rapoport, Kerpel, and Katz (1989) observed an 87 percent contribution rate when within-group discussion was allowed. Within-group discussion would thus seem to be beneficial. However, Bornstein (1992) recently discovered that within-group communication is only effective for step-level goods. When the groups are competing for a continuous good, between-group communication more often results in provision of the good.

Finally, we note that research on intergroup competition for a public good may be relevant to issues other than social dilemmas. Some researchers in the area of prejudice (e.g., Pettigrew, 1978; White, 1977; see also Hepworth & West, 1988) have argued that prejudicial attitudes occur because different categories of people are competing for the same scarce resources. An example would be male biases against female coworkers existing because the females took jobs away from other men. Since minimizing prejudice and discrimination involves fostering a sense of cooperation between various groups, the research on intergroup competition may suggest some useful approaches to the problem of prejudice.

Summary

Public goods are a pervasive part of society. Almost everyone has some degree of contact, and must make some decisions about, public goods. The topic has interested researchers in economics, political science, and sociology, as well as psychology.

Free riding, or the noncontribution to a public good, is presumed to have many causes. Among them are lack of self-efficacy, variables accompanying group size, and fear, either of being taken advantage of or of having one's efforts wasted. Many other variables have been hypothesized to affect free riding, but have not yet been adequately tested.

Attempts to minimize free riding include encouraging free discussion, offering guarantees and/or fair-share requirements, sanctioning noncontributors, and changing the method of contribution. Researchers continue to attempt to find solutions that could reasonably be implemented in real-world situations.

Social Traps

Consider each of the following situations:

1. Commercial fishers place a large number of nets in the ocean so as to catch greater numbers of a popular food fish.
2. Workers at a local fast-food restaurant take advantage of the company's ''free food for employees'' policy by giving free food to their friends.
3. University students fail to return copies of course textbooks that have been placed on reserve by the library until the end of the semester.

If you are an individual in any of these situations, you are clearly going to receive some immediate benefits. Your profits from fish sales will increase; you will strengthen your bonds of friendship;

you will not have to buy expensive textbooks. However, let's examine each of these instances from a long-term perspective. In the long run:

1. So many nets have been placed in the ocean that the fish are caught quicker than they can reproduce. As a result, the species quickly becomes extinct and the fishers go out of business.
2. The company suffers such a loss of food that it cancels the free-food policy.
3. The library gets so many complaints about missing readings that it stops reserving current course books.

In each of these situations, individuals acted so as to realize a small immediate gain, but in the long run, their collective behaviors were so detrimental that the group as a whole suffered a loss. Further, this eventual loss was much more negative than the short-term gain was positive. Any situation where short-term individual gains produce long-term group losses is known as a *social trap* (Cross & Guyer, 1980; Messick & Brewer, 1983; Platt, 1973).

As with public goods, the world is filled with social traps. An excellent example is water consumption. Tens of millions of Americans regularly consume vast amounts of water for their personal benefit (not only drinking, but also washing cars, watering lawns, etc.), but if a water table dries up, an entire city will suffer grave consequences.

In this chapter, we will first look at different types of social traps, and then narrow our focus to the most common type of trap, a *resource dilemma*. We will then discuss why people behave as they do in resource dilemma situations, and finally some techniques aimed at prolonging the life of the resource.

What Is a Social Trap?

A social (or collective) trap involves a group rather than a single individual in the consequences of the individual behaviors (Messick & Brewer, 1983). The classic example of such a trap is Hardin's (1968) "tragedy of the commons" that we looked at in Chapter 1. Behavior in situations like that described by Hardin are easily simulated in the laboratory using a paradigm known as a *resource dilemma* (Messick, Wilke, Brewer, Kramer, Zemke, & Lui, 1983). Almost all of the studies we will examine in this chapter are based on this paradigm.

The typical resource dilemma involves the following process. A group of subjects is given a resource pool (usually consisting of points) that they must manage. They may "harvest" as many points as they want out of the pool, up to a certain limit. After everyone has extracted some points, the pool is replenished at a set rate, which is usually related to the remaining pool size. Typically, the pool cannot be replenished to a level greater than the initial pool size, or the number of points in the pool before anyone has harvested. This would be analogous to trying to fit 12,000 gallons of water into a 10,000-gallon reservoir.

This process is repeated over a number of trials. Subjects are not allowed to discuss their decisions at any point in the game. Subjects receive some type of reward which increases as their individual harvests grow, but all are penalized if the pool "goes dry" (falls to 0 points), or alternatively is so low that not everyone could take the maximum harvest on the succeeding trial.

Finally, we should note that the resource dilemma paradigm does not require the experimenter to construct groups consisting entirely of "real" people. It is entirely possible to run a study where most of the "group members" are actually strategies programmed by the experimenter (Parker, Lui, Messick, Messick, Brewer, Kramer, Samuelson, & Wilke, (1983). Indeed, most of the experiments we will examine in this chapter used groups where only one member was an actual subject.

An example of how the process works might be helpful (see Figure 4.1). Consider a group of four subjects. We will abbreviate group size as N; thus, $N = 4$. We give them a "resource" pool consisting of 400 points to manage over a series of 15 trials; the initial pool size (IPS) is thus 400. Each group member can harvest up to 20 points on any given trial, and the pool is replenished at a rate of 10 percent of the remaining pool. We shall let r denote the replenishment rate; thus, $r = 0.1$. If, after replenishment, the pool drops below 80 points, then it is impossible for all persons to take a maximum harvest. When this happens, we will consider the pool to be "dry" and penalize all subjects by taking away half of the points that they have accumulated. In the typical experiment, subjects have complete knowledge of these criteria, except when the game ends (maximum number of trials).

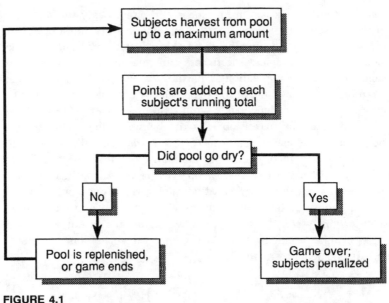

FIGURE 4.1
A resource dilemma experiment

Let's look at each person's behavior on the tenth trial. Suppose that after nine trials, each person has accumulated the following number of points:

Person A: 162 points.

Person B: 180 points.

Person C: 135 Points.

Person D: 108 points.

Also assume that after trial nine, the pool consists of 157 points. On trial ten, person A harvests 18 points; B, 20 points; C, 15 points; and D, 12 points. This leaves 92 points in the pool after all the harvests. The pool is replenished by adding 10 percent of the remaining pool back into the pool. Ten percent of 92 is 9.2. We don't want to deal with fractions, so we will round off and add in nine points. The pool for trial eleven, then, contains 101 points, and since pool size exceeds 80 points, the game continues.

This paradigm simulates many real-world processes quite closely, and is thus very attractive to researchers. Admittedly, actual replenishment rates are seldom constant; if the researcher was concerned about this feature, he/she could simply vary the rate randomly, by sampling values from a mathematical distribution, etc. A real-world example would be the fishing waters mentioned at the beginning of the chapter. The fishers can catch as many fish as they want, because the population is partially replenished whenever the fish reproduce; but if the species reproduces only at a given time of the year, the replenishment rate would vary.

This example makes obvious the nature of the dilemma in a social trap. How can one maximize reward *and* keep the pool from running out? In theory, there is an answer to this question. It is known as the concept of *optimal harvest level*. An optimal harvest level is an individual harvest value such that, if everyone were to make a harvest of this value, the pool would always be replenished to its original size. Thus, the pool would never run out, and each group member could continue to use the pool for as long as necessary. It is calculated as follows:

$$\text{Optimal} = \frac{(\text{IPS})(r)}{(N)(r + 1)} \qquad (1)$$

where IPS denotes initial pool size, N denotes group size, and r denotes replenishment rate. In our example above, IPS = 400, N = 4, and r = 0.1. Thus, the optimal harvest level for each subject is $(400 \times 0.1)/(4)(1.1) = 9.1$ (rounded to 9) points per person per trial. If, on the very first trial, each person would have harvested nine points, 364 points would have remained. Ten percent of 364 is 36.4, which rounds off to 36. Thirty-six added to 364 equals 400. As long as each person continues to take nine points per trial, the resource pool would never change. As we shall see, it is relatively rare for individuals to harvest at the optimal level.

Other Types of Traps
Before discussing research on resource dilemmas, we need to briefly mention some other types of traps. An *externality trap* (Cross & Guyer, 1980) occurs when some group members suffer the long-term consequences without having engaged in the short-term gratifying behaviors. An example would be a bicyclist who contracts a respiratory ailment from breathing smog. The bicyclist did nothing to contribute to the air pollution, but is nonetheless suffering the consequences. Most real-world collective traps involve externalities in some sense. From a social psychological point of view, however, externalities are uninteresting. We are primarily concerned with the behaviors of those who are producing the trap; the actions of "innocent bystanders" are not of primary theoretical significance.

A *social fence* (Messick & Brewer, 1983) is the opposite of a social trap. With a social fence, behaviors that would result in short-term individual losses will also produce long-term collective gains. A public good is a social fence. Contributing to a good's provision means a short-term loss (of money, time, etc.) to each individual, but a long-term collective gain of the good itself.

Another type of social trap is called *entrapment*. Entrapment (also referred to as "escalation," "sunk costs," or "throwing good money after bad") involves a continual commitment of resources to some action that is failing. There are many real instances of entrapment. For example, Staw (1981) discusses the person who continues to work toward a degree in a field for which almost no employment opportunities currently or will exist, and Teger (1980) cites the individual who continues to make expensive repairs on an old car. In both cases, the parties have invested in an action that did not produce positive outcomes in the past (past graduates did not get jobs, the car continued to break down), and is unlikely to do so in the future. We include entrapment as a social trap because the consequences of such behavior are often detrimental to some career group (the graduate must receive unemployment compensation, further burdening the federal budget; the driver does not buy a new car, hurting the auto industry). While entrapment behavior may, on the face of it, seem foolish, it is important to note that some researchers (e.g., Northcraft & Wolf, 1984) argue that entrapment is not necessarily irrational, if the cost in resources is small, or eventual success has a relatively high probability.

Many explanations for why entrapment occurs have been offered. Arkes and Blumer (1985) use a principle of prospect theory (Kahneman and Tversky, 1979): An uncertain gain is preferred over a sure loss. Ending one's commitment is a sure loss; continued commitment might produce eventual success. Thus, continuance is preferred over termination. Staw (1981) and Brockner, Rubin, and Lang (1981) argue for a self-presentation explanation. Giving up on a venture will make one look like a bad decision maker, because one's idea did not "work." On the other hand, if continued investment eventually produces success, one will look good and capable. Thus, individuals become entrapped because they want to present themselves in the best possible light. Finally, Conlon and Wolf (1980) suggest that entrapment is determined by decision strategy. According to this explanation, an individual whose decisions to continue are made intuitively, rather than by explicitly examining past expenditures and calculating future costs, is much more likely to become entrapped.

Interestingly, Garland, Sandefur, and Rogers (1990) found that experts may not fall prey to entrapment. They asked petroleum geologists whether they would build another oil exploration well in a field given that one, two, or three previous wells in that field had been dry. As the number of dry wells increased, the geologists were decreasingly likely to build another, a pattern opposite to entrapment. Clearly, much more work is needed in this area.

Finally, we take note of the most basic social trap, which involves one and only one person. Known as an *individual trap* (Messick & Brewer, 1983) or *temporal trap* (Messick & McClelland, 1983), it is a situation in which a person engages in an immediately gratifying behavior, only to suffer later consequences from the same behavior. An excellent example of an individual trap is smoking. A smoker receives the immediate, pleasurable sensation produced by nicotine (or, after becoming addicted, avoids unpleasant nicotine withdrawal); however, smoking also greatly increases the chances that the person will suffer from lung cancer later in life. While interesting, the temporal trap lacks the social element that we are interested in here (and is not technically a social dilemma because group size is less than two).

Behavior in a Social Trap

What should a person do when faced with a resource dilemma? This is not an easy question to answer. Consider a water table. Some states have been plagued by droughts in recent years. Governments in these states have told their residents that they must cut back on their use of water, or risk running out altogether. Most people would like to plan for the future, but most people also like a clean car, a green lawn, and long showers. On the other hand, important industries like farming, and popular diversions like golf courses, use tremendous amounts of water; maybe we should compensate for them by cutting our own use of water. Of course, if everyone else is using a lot of water, maybe we should also, so we don't get ''cheated'' out of our fair share.

Clearly, a member of a group faced with a resource dilemma has a number of factors to consider before deciding how to behave. Messick and his colleagues have studied in great detail how these factors affect one's behavior in a social trap. They hypothesize that an individual group member has at least three, often conflicting, motives in a social trap (Messick et al., 1983). First, people want to act in their own best interests. It is most convenient to shower everday, so people should do so. This is the individually rational way to act, so it should not surprise you that this motive is present. Second, a person wants to use the resource pool wisely. An example of this behavior would be to "counteract" the choices of others. If most other people are overconsuming the resource, the smart thing to do would be to cut back on one's own usage so that the total amount of resource consumed remains the same. Thus, if two people each use 100 gallons of water a week, one should cut his/her consumption to 90 gallons if the other suddenly raises his/hers to 110. Finally, there are conformity pressures to make choices similar to those of other group members. In other words, if everyone else is conserving water, you should too. These motives frequently come into conflict, and the resolution of the conflict can be affected by a number of variables.

Responsible Harvesting

The motive to act responsibly is usually studied by showing subjects that their fellow group members are "overusing" or "underusing" the resource pool. An example of such information is illustrated in Table 4.1. Overuse, of course, means that the others are taking too much of the resource and it will soon be depleted. Underusing, or taking too little of a resource, means that individuals are not maximizing their own personal gain; in other words, their harvests are less than the optimal harvest level. Underuse can sometimes be as detrimental as overuse, especially if a resource is perishable. For example, grain in a food cooperative will rot if it is not consumed quickly enough.

As we said earlier, a person who wants to act responsibly should make harvests that counteract, or are opposite to those of the others. That is, one should make small harvests if everyone else is overusing, and large harvests if everyone is underusing. In fact, this is exactly how subjects in resource dilemmas behave. Almost all studies of resource dilemmas show that overuse leads subjects to

TABLE 4.1 Examples of Overuse and Underuse

Condition	Pool Size on Trial						
	1	2	3	4	5	6	7
Overuse	400	352	299	241	177	107	30
Underuse	400	400	395	400	398	399	400

make smaller harvests than underuse (e.g., Rutte, Wilke, & Messick, 1987; Samuelson & Messick, 1986a, 1986b; Samuelson, Messick, Rutte, & Wilke, 1984). The desire to act responsibly, then, seems to be well-established.

Conformity

Conformity pressures can be studied by varying the range of harvests of the other group members. A typical set of values is shown in Table 4.2 for two groups of six persons each, where I and II denote the two groups. Note that, in both conditions, the mean harvest is the same (13.8), but the range (variability) of harvests is much larger in Group II than in Group I. If conformity is a factor, the conformity pressures should increase as the range of harvests made by other group members narrows. This is because, as the choices of other members become more similar, the person may come to perceive and develop a norm or standard for a "correct" amount to harvest, and he/she will be hesitant to deviate from that norm. By contrast, if choices vary widely, then there is probably no single harvest that the group "expects" each member to make. A person who is in Group I, then, should feel much more pressure, and consequently make a harvest much closer to 14 points than a person in Group II.

Individual choices do seem to be affected by the range of others' harvests, though the nature of the relationship is not exactly clear. Samuelson, Messick, Rutte, and Wilke (1984) showed that the range alone can sufficiently increase or decrease conformity pressure. In their studies, subjects believed that they were playing a resource dilemma with other subjects; in reality, the other "group members" were sets of choices that were predetermined by the experimenters. The range of harvests of the "group members" was either large or small, in a manner similar to that shown in Table 4.2. Subjects played for ten trials (though they did not know this exact figure) or until the pool ran out. At the end of the trials, there was a chance that the subject's accumulated points would be converted into money at a five-cent-per-point rate. Samuelson and colleagues found that subjects whose fellow "group members" made a narrow range of choices showed harvest values much closer to the group average than did those who experienced a wide range. When variability was high, subjects tended to act in their own best interests and harvested at a rate higher than the average.

TABLE 4.2 Broad and Narrow Harvest Ranges

| Two Groups | Harvests of Other Group Members | | | | | | |
	A	B	C	D	E	Mean	Range
I	10	13	13	15	18	13.8	8
II	4	5	11	22	27	13.8	23

Other studies have shed further light on the range-conformity relation. Samuelson and Messick (1986a, 1986b) showed that variance interacts with use. In those studies, high variance led to large individual harvests only when others were using the pool responsibly; chronic overuse of the pool led subjects to make smaller-than-average harvests, even when variance was high. Samuelson and Messick (1986a) and Samuelson et al. (1984) found that variance interacts with the number of trials. High variance produces individual harvests greater than the group norm, but only after a period of time. Taken together, these studies suggest that conformity pressure operates only when a resource is not overused. If the resource is being rapidly depleted, individuals tend to conserve, regardless of what others are doing.

Overuse or underuse of a resource is not necessarily caused by the individuals consuming it. The resource itself can sometimes produce over/underuse. For example, if six cooks are given 100 pounds of apples per month, it is likely the apples will go bad before they can all be used. The pool of apples has been underused, but not because of any deficient behaviors on the part of the group members. Similarly, if the same six cooks are given only eight apples per month, the apple pool will probably be exhausted very quickly, though not through any fault of the individuals.

It is possible that conformity pressures are affected by whether you attribute over/underuse to fellow group members or the resource itself. Rutte and colleagues (1987) examined this relation. They conducted a study using a procedure very similar to the one described earlier in this section, except that subjects played for money rather than points. Subjects believed they were part of a real group engaged in a resource dilemma. In reality, the behaviors of other ''group members'' were simulated by the experimenters. Subjects were led to believe that their ''group'' was either overusing or underusing the resource pool by receiving bogus feedback. This feedback indicated that other members were either harvesting a lot of money (overuse), or little money (underuse). Further, subjects were told that the over/underuse was caused by either the choices of their fellow "group members" (e.g., others were being greedy) or the initial pool size being too small/large (e.g., the pool was too small for so many people to use). Rutte *et al.* found that subjects tended to conform to the choices of others when over/underuse could be attributed to other group members, but acted responsibly when over/underuse was believed to be the result of the environment (pool size).

Liebrand, Wilke, and colleagues have argued that individuals in social trap situations want to establish a *reciprocal relationship* with other group members, so that one's choices tend to match those of others; (Liebrand, Jansen, Rijken, & Suhre, 1986; Liebrand, Wilke, Vogel, & Wolters, 1986; Wilke & Braspenning, 1989; see also Schroeder, Jensen, Reed, Sullivan, & Schwab, 1983). This desire shows up as early as the very first trial. Wilke and Braspenning (1989) asked subjects, before they made their harvest choices on Trial 1, how many points they thought the other members would harvest on Trial 1. They found that the correlation between a person's Trial 1 choice and the expected choices of others on Trial 1 was 0.83. Wilke and Braspenning did not solicit any personal reactions from subjects, so it is not clear whether subjects truly desired to conform, or were acting strategically to elicit cooperation from other group members in a manner similar to tit-for-tat, or were simply projecting their own behavior onto the others.

Behavior Over Time

We saw in Chapter 2 that subjects in prisoner's dilemma games make fewer cooperative choices as the game goes on. All studies of resource dilemmas are multi-trial games. It is thus logical to ask whether, as in the prisoner's dilemma, behavior changes over time. Many studies show that, as in the NPD, harvests tend to increase over trials (e.g., Messick *et al.*, 1983; Samuelson & Messick, 1986a; Samuelson *et al.*, 1984). As the dilemma progresses, subjects are acting more for their own personal benefit (greed), and less for the group good, by taking larger portions of the pool. We have seen, however, that it is also very common for time and use to interact (e.g., Samuelson & Messick, 1986a, 1986b; Samuelson *et al.*, 1984). In these studies, mean harvests increased over time only when others were not overusing the pool. People whose fellow group members repeatedly took near-maximum amounts of points tended to maintain a consistent level of harvesting, or even decreased their harvests. Messick *et al.*, (1983) found that time interacted with both use and variance; harvests increased only when the pool was not overused *and* the range of others' choices was high. The conclusion to be drawn here (with exceptions: see Samuelson, 1991) seems to be that individuals will increase their harvests as the game progresses, but only if others are not abusing the pool.

Complex Behavior in a Social Trap

We have seen that different, often conflicting motives we may face in a resource dilemma (own best interests, responsible pool use, conformity) can interact in many ways. It may seem that there is little consistency among the myriad of results we have discussed in this part of the chapter. In fact, the results do suggest one general conclusion: Prediction of harvesting behavior (cooperation) is extremely difficult without first analyzing the task confronting the group. In order to make predictions about a particular person's behavior, we would need to know whether that person was aware of the choices of others, whether he/she monitored the resource's changing size, and so on. In addition, researchers continue to test other social factors that may partially affect such behavior.

Solving Resource Dilemmas

A large portion of research on social traps, and resource dilemmas in particular, has been devoted to how to "solve" them, that is, to identify techniques or interventions that will maintain the pool near its original, or some other, long term level. Research has focused on two different types of solutions: *structural* solutions, or techniques that involve changing the structure of the dilemma in some way, and *individual* solutions, or attempts to alter individual choice behavior (Messick & Brewer, 1983).

Structural Solutions

Studies of structural alterations have mainly centered around two techniques: changing the methods by which group members choose their harvests and partitioning the resource. The former has received considerable attention from researchers, while the latter is a new approach. We will look at each in turn.

Free-Choice versus Leaders

Messick, Samuelson, and colleagues have investigated the efficiency and popularity of a "leader-based" rather than "free-choice" means of harvesting. Under a *leader-based system,* one member of the group is selected to act as the leader, and harvests for each person in the group. Under a *free-choice system,* each person decides his/her own harvest size. The method used to study structural change is a simple one. Typically, subjects are asked to play two sessions of a resource dilemma game. The first session is conducted in the manner we are familiar with. After its completion, subjects are asked if they would prefer to change the decision-making structure for the second session. If so, they are usually given a number of structures from which to choose. Typically, subjects have three options: (1) choose a leader who will distribute the points; (2) each person receives a portion of the resource for his/her personal use (known as *privatization*), or (3) place a cap on harvest size.

Who Wants to Change?

A consistent finding is that subjects whose group overused the pool are much more likely to prefer to change the decision structure (Messick *et al.,* 1983; Samuelson & Messick, 1986a, 1986b; Samuelson *et al.,* 1984). (Recall that in these studies, subjects played with simulated "group members" and that the experimenters systematically manipulated the range of choices and the over/underuse of the pool.) Samuelson *et al.* (1984) argue that this is the result of an attributional process. Subjects believe that any system that allows others to overuse the pool must be a faulty one, and therefore should be changed. Along these lines, it is interesting to note that subjects who experienced high variance in the choices of others expressed dissatisfaction with the game, but were likely to prefer to maintain the free-choice system. In this situation, subjects may be attributing fault not to the system but to a few greedy individuals, and thus see no reason to change the system. Similarly, Samuelson (1991) found that subjects voted to change the decision structure (to a new leader-based system) when they believed that depletion was caused by an inherent difficulty in maintaining the pool (they were told that almost no group had successfully managed the pool to that point), but not when they believed depletion was the result of greedy group members. His results suggest that individuals will desire a change not only when they believe the current system is inadequate, but also when they believe a change will be effective at enforcing cooperation.

What Kind of Change?

We know the conditions under which group members are most likely to want to change the decision structure. But, will they necessarily view a leader-based system as the best one to adopt if they have other options? The evidence regarding this question is somewhat mixed. Samuelson and Messick (1986a) had subjects play a standard resource dilemma game. After the session ended, subjects were told that they would play a second session, and had the option of changing the decision structure. Some subjects had the option of switching to a leader system; some, to privatize the pool, with all group members receiving an equal portion; and some, to a proportional division system where point allotments were tied to one's first-session harvest total (i.e., the higher one's total harvest was, the larger one's second-session harvest would be). They found that subjects with the leader option most frequently voted to change the structure. In a second study, in which all subjects considered all options, Samuelson and Messick (1986b) asked subjects to rank each of the above three alternatives in terms of preference; interestingly, the equal-division option, not the leader option, proved to be most popular. In fact, Rutte and Wilke (1985) showed that a leader-based system is very *unpopular* when members also have the option of having the group itself, rather than a single individual, decide the size of harvest allotments (e.g., majority or unanimity rules). Thus, it seems that leader selection is not a structural change preferred by many individuals.

Who Should Lead?

Groups that do adopt a leader-based decision-making structure must also select one member to act as leader. Given this, whom do individuals think should act as leader? Surprisingly few people vote for themselves. For example, only 35 percent of Messick *et al.*'s (1983) subjects chose themselves, and only 38 percent of Samuelson *et al.*'s (1984) did so. For the most part, individuals seem to prefer that others make the allocation decisions. Recall that no communication is allowed during the resource dilemma game. Because of this, individual perceptions of others must be based entirely on harvesting behaviors. Messick *et al.* found that the group member who received the most leader votes tended to have accumulated a moderate amount of points during the first session. This suggests that subjects want a leader who is aware of, and harvests at, near-optimal levels. In Samuelson *et al.*, votes were dependent on previous pool use. If the pool had been overused, an individual with a low point total was popular; conversely, pool underuse led to the selection of a person who had a very high point total. The conclusion here is that subjects want a leader who will "counteract" the inadequacies of the previous session. In both studies, subject choices were logical given the results of the first session. Even without interaction, subjects thus seem to be able to sensibly choose a leader.

Partitionment

A more recent attempt to structurally alter the resource involves partitionment, the division of the resource into discrete units. This approach is based on cognitive heuristics. A *heuristic* can be thought of an intuitive strategy for simplifying a cognitively complex problem (Kahneman, Slovic, & Tversky, 1982). For example, when a person uses an "anchoring" heuristic, he/she estimates some value by basing the estimate on a similar value that is familiar to him/her. If you wanted to determine the average grade point for all the students at your school, you could certainly obtain every student's transcript and calculate the mean, but this would be incredibly difficult. It would be much easier to assume that most students are like yourself, and thus have GPA's similar to yours. Using this logic, if your GPA is a 2.8, you might estimate the average grade point to be 2.7. You have thus used your GPA as an "anchor" to which you tied your estimate, and simplified a difficult problem. A common, mistaken assumption about heuristics is that, because they are a "shortcut," they produce poor decisions and should be avoided. While it is true that heuristic decisions are often not as accurate as actually working through the problem, heuristic estimates are usually good enough to suffice. If your school's average GPA were around 2.5, then your estimate would be acceptable for most purposes.

Allison and Messick (1990) have suggested that people often rely on heuristics to help them decide how much to harvest. Specifically, they argue that these individuals use an "equality" heuristic, which prescribes that everyone should harvest the same amount. Equality is a prominent social norm, commonly used in many other social situations (Deutsch, 1975; Harris & Joyce, 1980), so it would seem likely that it would figure into resource management as well. Indeed, an earlier study by Rutte, Wilke, and Messick (1987) presented data that many people prefer equal division of a resource. Since most people consider equal division to be a fair means of allocation (Messick & Sentis, 1979), it would seem to be preferable for group members to use this heuristic.

There are some situations, however, where it is difficult to apply an equality rule. Allison, McQueen, and Schaerfl (1992) suggested that the partition of the resource is crucial to equality. If my four-person group has eight 10-gallon buckets of water, it is easy for us to apply the equality rule: each person gets two buckets, or 20 gallons. But what if we are given one 80-gallon bucket? Without a measuring device, it is virtually impossible for us to ensure that each person uses exactly 20 gallons. Further, in the former situation there is no way I can cheat without being caught, but in the latter instance it would be quite easy to be greedy. Who could tell if I used 25, rather than 20, gallons? Allison and colleagues thus predicted that the equality rule would be applied less often when the resource is not easily divisible. To test this, they gave three– and twelve–person groups one of two resources to manage: A number of wooden blocks (6 or 24 respectively), or a bucket of sand (6 or 24 pounds). It is easy to give all members an equal number of blocks, but difficult (again, without a measuring device) to distribute equal amounts of sand. Allison and colleagues predicted that "block" groups would more often use the equality rule than "sand" groups. This is exactly what happened. Seventy-six percent of "block" groups used equality; only 40 percent of "sand" groups did. Further, members of twelve-person "sand" groups took on average more than 4.5 pounds of sand; equal division would give them 2 pounds. By contrast, members of three-person "sand" groups were very good at dividing the resource (1.8 pounds). As you might expect, both "block" groups harvested very close to the equal value—1.8 and 2.1 blocks, respectively. Not all resources can be neatly divided, of course, but doing so for those resources with which it can be done would seem to help inhibit overconsumption, particularly in larger groups.

Individual Solutions

A second technique for "solving" resource dilemmas involves altering individual selection behavior rather than the resource structure itself. In contrast to structural solutions, a number of different *individual solutions* have been investigated. We will look at some of these solutions here.

Communication
We saw in the previous chapter that allowing group members to discuss a public goods dilemma results in dramatic increases in cooperation. Could communication have similar effects in a social trap?

Early research (Brechner, 1977; Edney & Harper, 1978; Jorgenson & Papciak, 1981) suggested that it could. Liebrand (1984) conducted a resource dilemma experiment in which half of the groups were allowed to discuss the task, the other half could not. The exact size of the pool (consisting of money) was unknown, but groups did know that the pool would fall within a certain specified range (from $95 to $115). Each subject requested some amount of money from the pool. After all members made a request, the requests were added to yield a total request. Pool size was randomly selected from within the specified range. If the pool was larger than the total request, all members got their harvests, but if total request exceeded pool size, no payoffs were given.

Liebrand found that discussion groups were much more effective pool managers than groups that had no verbal interaction. Collectively, the best course of action is to request individual amounts such that the total request is less than the range minimum of $95. That way, the pool will always exceed requests, and a payoff is guaranteed. In fact, 70 percent of Liebrand's communicating groups used exactly this strategy. The likelihood of *any* communicating group receiving a payoff was 94 percent. By contrast, none of the noncommunicating groups used this strategy; the likelihood of their receiving a payoff was only 54 percent. One group never received any payoffs.

Messick, Allison, and Samuelson (1988) also found face-to-face discussion to be beneficial. Using a paradigm similar to the one employed by Liebrand, their subjects used free discussion to identify optimal behaviors and to coordinate their choices accordingly. Ninety percent of their communicating groups received payoffs; only 20 percent of noncommunicating groups did. Thus, discussion clearly seems to be effective at improving resource pool management. Recall from Chapter 3 that discussion also proved to be very useful for increasing contribution rates in public goods games. Discussion, then, seems to be an effective method of enhancing cooperation regardless of the type of dilemma.

Experience

A feature common to the laboratory research we have discussed so far is that the task was relatively unfamiliar to all subjects. It is highly unlikely that any of the subjects had engaged in anything like an experimental resource dilemma before they entered the laboratory. In the real world, however, our encounters with real social traps are continual, and we may benefit from this experience by being able to make more informed decisions. The natural question to ask is, "What if laboratory subjects had previous experience with an experimental resource dilemma?"

Allison and Messick (1985) had subjects manage two consecutive sets of resource dilemmas. In the first session, subjects managed the pool either individually (i.e., each was the only person harvesting from the pool) or as part of a group. For the second session, all persons worked in groups: groups from the first session were kept intact, while first-session individuals were grouped together. Allison and Messick found that groups composed of experienced individuals were significantly better at maintaining their pool in the second session than were experienced groups. Interestingly, experienced groups were no better than inexperienced groups at pool maintenance. Allison and Messick also showed that individual experience proved more beneficial as group size increased. Thus, people do seem to be able to learn efficient pool management strategies, but only by being solely responsible for the pool's maintenance. However, this individualized training seems to transfer to group management settings.

Stern (1976) tested the benefits of explicitly educating subjects about the likely consequences of their various choice options. His subjects received either basic pre-game information regarding the nature of the game, or a complete pre-game description of how choices would affect the life of the pool. Not surprisingly, groups that had received the full information maintained their pool significantly longer than the basic-information groups. Stern also gave some subjects periodic "spot messages" that provided cues as to the optimal pattern of choices. Interestingly, such hints had no effect on individual harvests. Similarly, Orbell and Dawes (1981) observed increases in cooperative behavior when subjects were given a pre-game lecture regarding the benefits of cooperation. Education seems to be effective only when it is fully and completely provided at the outset.

Taken together, these studies indicate that experience, either practical or formal, can produce positive results regarding resource conservation. However, not just any experience will suffice; attention must be paid to the type and form of experience given.

Social Identity

One factor that may be involved in harvest decisions is trust. To what extent do you think others will try to take advantage of you if you choose responsibly? If you are very distrustful, the reasonable course of action to take is to make large harvests on every trial. On the other hand, if you have faith that your fellow group members will not exploit your good intentions, your harvests should be at or near the optimal level. In fact, Messick *et al.* (1983) found that as the resources dwindled, high-trust individuals did reduce their harvests, while low-trusters increased their harvests. This suggests an interesting question: "Is it possible to increase a person's general trust of others?"

The concept of *social identity* is a pervasive one in groups research. Social identity can be thought of as the extent to which you consider yourself a member of some group(s). Someone with a *collective social identity* would think of him/herself primarily as a group member (e.g., "I am a New Yorker," "I am an Illini"). By contrast, a person with an *individual social identity* downplays his/her membership in social groups. An individual with a collective social identity will place greater emphasis on group rather than individual gains; the reverse is true for individual social identity (Brewer, 1979, 1981; Kramer & Brewer, 1986).

Many researchers (e.g., Dawes, 1990) believe that social identity is a crucial concept for understanding why people cooperate and how to improve cooperation. Recall from Chapter 2 that "individuation" and "ingroup identity" have been suggested as possible explanations for cooperative behavior in the prisoner's dilemma. It is possible that social identity has similar effects on harvesting behavior. Brewer (1981) and Messick and Brewer (1983) have suggested that instilling a superordinate social identity in group members should increase feelings of trust, and in turn optimal harvesting. A group whose members feel a strong sense of collective identity should thus be much more efficient in maintaining a resource than a group whose members are individually-oriented.

Kramer and Brewer (1984) and Brewer and Kramer (1986) tested this hypothesis using resource dilemma and public goods paradigms in which the other "group members" were simulated by the experimenter. In a series of studies, they systematically manipulated the level of social identity of subjects and compared the harvesting behaviors of collective-identity versus individual-identity subjects. Social identity was typically manipulated by taking advantage of naturally occurring categories. For example, in one study all subjects were psychology majors. The subjects were told that the other "group members" were economics majors. To instill a collective identity, some subjects were told that the purpose of the experiment was to compare the performance of university students against nonstudent groups. Subjects in the "individual identity" condition were told that the purpose of the experiment was to compare psychology majors and economics majors.

Kramer and Brewer found that individuals for which a collective identity was strongest were significantly better at managing the resource than subordinate-identity subjects. This efficiency was independent of group size; collective-identity subjects were better than individual-identity subjects even when the "group" was as large as 32 members. The studies also produced two curious results. First, Kramer and Brewer (1984) found no evidence linking group identity to trust. That is, those with a collective identity were not necessarily more trusting of others than were individual-identity subjects. Second, Brewer and Kramer (1986) found collective identity to have a much weaker effect on behavior in a public goods situation, particularly when the group was large. They explain this latter result by suggesting that in a large group, the riskiness of public goods (keeping one's contribution and gambling that enough others will contribute) can be diffused; in other words, the larger the group, the more likely it is that a sufficient number of others will contribute. Instilling a collective identity only makes one more aware that the group is large, and in turn that enough other contributors probably exist. If we think a sufficient number of others will contribute, there is no reason for us to do so.

The extent to which one thinks of oneself as a "group member" thus seems to have some effect on behavior, at least in social trap situations. If we also consider the "individuation" research discussed in Chapter 2, it seems that social identity is an important component of cooperative behavior.

Punishment
Finally, what if individual group members were punished for overconsumption? We have seen that punishment is a potentially effective technique for controlling free riding in public goods situations (Yamagishi, 1986, a & b). It is possible that punishment will also inhibit individuals from harvesting excessive amounts of a resource. Bell, Petersen, and Hautaluoma (1989) tested this hypothesis. Their subjects played a resource dilemma game that was slightly modified: on any given trial, subjects had the option of either harvesting from the pool or stealing from another group member's accumulated points. Subjects were told that if they harvested or stole an excessive amount of points, there was a probability (25 percent or 75 percent) that they would be penalized by having some points subtracted

from their own accumulated total. Bell and colleagues found that, compared to subjects for whom there was no penalty, the presence of potential punishment significantly prolonged the life of the resource. Interestingly, the harsher (75 percent) penalty did not produce a longer resource life than the lenient (25 percent) penalty. This suggests that the mere threat of a penalty is sufficient to induce conservation; the severity of that threat is of little consequence. However, the presence of the threat had a negative side effect: subjects became more willing to steal points from others. Conversely, attempting to inhibit stealing with punishment led to more frequent overharvesting. It is not clear what effect punishment would have on subjects for whom stealing is not an option; future research may address this issue.

Summary

Social traps, like public goods, are a common element of our society. We have seen that there are many different types of traps, but perhaps the most common is the collective trap. Researchers studying collective traps often use the "resource dilemma" laboratory paradigm. There seem to be three general, often conflicting motives underlying harvesting behavior: to act in one's own best interest, to conform, and to act responsibly. Research has not yet established which motive, if any, dominates the others.

Researchers interested in devising techniques for minimizing overconsumption of a resource have tested both structural and behavioral solutions to the problem. Structural solutions usually involve changing the decision-making process or dividing the resource into discrete portions. By contrast, many different behavioral solutions have been examined. Some of the potentially important solutions include communication, giving group members experience with resource management, enhancing group identity, and punishing overconsumers.

Social Values

In Chapter 2, we saw that an important factor that affects behavior in the prisoner's dilemma is one's general predisposition to respond in a certain way. Though this predisposition is alternatively referred to as a motivational orientation, social motive, or value orientation, they are perhaps most widely known as *social values;* hence, this is the term we shall use in this chapter. Social values have received a great deal of research attention, especially in the last decade; however, there are many unresolved issues regarding social values. For these reasons, it is fruitful for us to look at social values in some detail.

    Many researchers believe that social values represent one component of personality. Some believe that social values are more reflective of one's attitudes, but research in this area generally does not support this assertion (Baxter, 1972). Aspects of our personality are generally thought to be more or less fixed, and our basic personality is not expected to change very much during our lifetime

TABLE 5.1 Some Other Social Values

Value	Choice pattern
Aggression	Minimize other person's payoff
Altruism	Maximize other person's payoff
Equality	Minimize difference in payoffs
Martyrdom	Maximize other, minimize own payoff

(Mischel, 1968). Further, personalities are considered to be quite stable across a wide variety of situations (Hogan & Nicholson, 1988; Mischel, 1968). If you are extroverted and outgoing, you will probably be so for your entire life, and you will be so regardless of whether you are with other extroverts or some more introverted people. (As with other aspects of human behavior, there are of course exceptions to both the fixedness and stability of personality.) Given this, we shall define a social value as a preference for a specific pattern of outcomes, in a setting of outcome interdependence, that is consistent over time (McClintock, 1977; McClintock & Liebrand, 1988).

We saw in Chapter 2 that Messick and McClintock (1968) identified a number of different social values (see also Greisinger & Livingston, 1973). Many other specific values have been proposed since then. However, there are three values that are common to most, if not all, social value studies:

1. A *cooperator* attempts to maximize the total units accumulated by the group on any given trial. This is usually referred to as maximizing joint gain.
2. A *competitor* attempts to maximize the difference between his/her personal outcome and the outcome of others on any given trial. This is known as maximizing relative gain.
3. An *individualist* is solely concerned with obtaining the most units for him/herself on any given trial. The individualist is not concerned with the outcome of others. This is known as maximizing own gain.

Table 5.1 summarizes some other social values that have been mentioned in one or more studies.

To see how these different values would affect choice in a social dilemma, consider the prisoner's dilemma shown in Table 5.2.

TABLE 5.2 A Two-Person Prisoner's Dilemma

	Other's Choice	
	C	D
Subject's C	6, 6	2, 8
Choice D	8, 2	4, 4

Note. In earlier chapters we distinguished the outcomes of the row and column players with a diagonal "slash" (line) in each cell of the payoff table (see Figures 1.1 and 1.2 as examples). We shall hereafter use a comma to distinguish the outcomes of the two players; thus, the first and second entries in each cell represent the outcomes of the row and column players, respectively.

If our subject is a Cooperator, he/she should choose C, because it can produce the most total points (12) if the other person also cooperates. If he/she is a Competitor, he/she should choose D, because the difference between Own Payoff and Other's Payoff (6) will be largest if the other person chooses C.

Assessment of Social Values

A major issue in personality research is how to assess the particular personality construct of interest. Because personalities are so complex, it is difficult to measure specific aspects of an individual's personality. As a result, most studies of social values have concentrated on developing instruments that accurately reflect a person's choice preferences. A variety of instruments have been developed, and we shall look at most of them in some detail. We shall then turn our attention to some empirical research on social values.

Measures of Social Values

Many techniques have been derived to assess one's social value orientation. We will look here at the major techniques. Then, we will discuss some measures of other individual difference traits that may be related to social values.

The Decomposed Prisoner's Dilemma

It was originally believed that an individual's social value orientation could be inferred from his/her pattern of choices in a standard two-person, two-choice game like the prisoner's dilemma (McClintock & van Avermaet, 1982). There are, however, many problems

TABLE 5.3 A Decomposed Prisoner's Dilemma

	Combination (choices)		
	A	B	C
Own payoff	6	5	7
Other's payoff	6	1	4

with this procedure. The most serious is that it is impossible to make value distinctions finer than "cooperator" or "noncooperator." In a prisoner's dilemma, most of a Cooperator's choices would of course be cooperative, but so would an Altruist's; if we observed a subject making mostly cooperative choices, we would have no way of knowing if the person was a Cooperator or Altruist.

To address this problem, McClintock, Kuhlman, and colleagues (Kuhlman, Camac, & Cunha, 1986; Kuhlman & Marshello, 1975; Kuhlman & Wimberley, 1976; McClintock, Messick, Kuhlman, & Campos, 1973; Messick & McClintock, 1968) have proposed using decomposed prisoner's dilemmas, or DPDs, to assess values. One basic DPD is shown in Table 5.3. [Liebrand (1984) has also created a DPD procedure, commonly known as the "ring measure," that uses a geometric logic of axes and vectors to identify social values.] The subject is told that he/she and another subject will receive some amount of a resource (typically money or points). The subject must decide how the resource should be allocated. He/she must choose between three (or sometimes two) different combinations of resource allocations to self and other.

The subject's preference should be affected by his/her social value orientation. A Cooperator should prefer combination A, because it produces more total points (12) than combinations B or C. A Competitor should be attracted to combination B, because the difference between own and other's payoff is largest with this combination. Finally, the Individualist should choose combination C, because it gives him/her more points than A or B.

In order to determine the person's value orientation, a subject is asked to respond to a number of different DPDs and the choices are tallied. The choice that occurs at least 66 percent of the time is considered to reflect that person's social value. For example, suppose a subject completes 24 DPDs. After tallying her choices, we observe that she made 19 competitive choices, 4 individualistic choices, and 1 cooperative choice. Since 79 percent of her choices were competitive, we would conclude that she is a Competitor. Any person who does not meet this "66 percent consistency" rule is considered to be unclassifiable.

Mathematical Approaches

Some researchers have attempted to use mathematical models to determine an individual's value orientation. In fact, one of the earliest attempts at assessing social values was a model proposed by Sawyer (1966). If we let P and O denote outcomes for self and the other person, he defined: (a) cooperation as the motive to maximize (P + O); (b) competition as the motive to maximize (P − O); and (c) individualism as the motive to maximize P. Human behavior, of course, is rarely pure; to account for this, Sawyer proposed a mathematical weight a which could range from −1.0 to +1.0, to represent the relative importance of the motive to maximize P and O. Employing this weight, he proposed the following general equation as a measure of social values:

$$\text{Orientation} = P + aO \tag{1}$$

For Cooperators, a will be positive; for Competitors, negative; and for Individualists, zero. For example, if we substitute $a = +1$ in Equation 1, we have: orientation = P + 0; if we substitute $a = -1$, orientation = P − O; and if we substitute $a = 0$, orientation = P. Of course, a can be any value between −1 and +1, and a person's orientation could be any combination of two types of orientations. For example, if $a = +0.50$, orientation = P + (.50)O, and such a person's social value orientation would be halfway between cooperation and individualism.

To identify a person's social value orientation, the experimenter need simply to determine the person's value of a. Sawyer devised two means to determine a: a direct method of having the subject rate, on a scale from −1 to +1, various outcomes for self (P) and Other (O), and an indirect method, in which the subject is asked to rank various Self-Other combinations. Data from the two methods are then combined to obtain a value for a. Unfortunately, the means by which these data are combined is quite cumbersome and complicated, and consequently we shall not illustrate them here.

An alternate technique that is quite mathematical has been proposed by Knight and Dubro (1984). This method requires the experimenter to calculate a regression equation for each subject and conduct a cluster analysis on the resulting data. Basically, *cluster analysis* is a technique for identifying groups of subjects with similar preferences. (An excellent discussion of the mathematics of cluster analysis can be found in Arabie, Carroll, & DeSarbo, 1987.)

Like the DPD, the subject's task is very simple and easily understood. The subject is told to imagine that he/she and another person will each be receiving some amount of money between zero and six dollars. The amount of money he/she and the other person receives will not necessarily be the same amount. The subject's task is to consider all possible pairs of own/other payoff combinations between zero-zero and six-six, and to rate the desirability of each pair on a seven-point scale (e.g., "On a scale of 1 to 7, 1 being not desirable, how desirable is the following combination: Three dollars to you, one dollar to the other person."). These ratings are then cluster analyzed to identify subjects who prefer similar payoff combinations. Each cluster is assumed to contain subjects who share the same predominant social value.

A third approach that is mathematical in nature has been proposed by Wyer (1969, 1971). Wyer rejected the idea of assigning specific labels to individual preferences. Rather, he described interpersonal outcome preferences in terms of *utility*. Utility can be thought of as the value one places on something. For example, if you get more enjoyment out of a stereo than a videocassette player, we would say that your utility for the stereo is higher than it is for the VCR. Wyer argued that one has a definite, measurable utility for every possible combination of Own-Other outcomes. He derived a complex regression equation, incorporating payoff to self and other, that produces a measure of the utility of a particular payoff combination for a specific person. In a series of studies, Wyer found this equation to be very predictive of payoff utilities.

Problems with Social Value Measures

While quite popular, these measures of social values are not without their problems. For example, a subject must meet a certain criterion before he/she can be examined in detail. A subject who does not show "66 percent consistency" with a DPD, or who fails to have any significant regression values, must be discarded. This problem is not uncommon; almost all published studies using the DPD have analyzed only a subset of the original subject population, e.g., Maki and McClintock (1983) report 30 percent attrition. Subject loss with individualized regression will usually be much lower; for example, Knight and Dubro report losing only 3 percent of their subjects. However, a researcher who does not have access to a large subject pool may not be able to afford much attrition.

Additional problems with the mathematical approaches are their basis in advanced statistical techniques and labor intensiveness. Cluster analysis is a somewhat uncommon analytical tool, at least among social psychologists, and as such many researchers may not have the understanding, ability, or computational power necessary to use the individualized regression method. Similarly, calculating regression equations for each member of a subject pool can be very time-consuming. While Sawyer's model is quite simple algebraically, the means of obtaining a single value for a is very complex. The researcher who does not have adequate resources (time, assistance) at his/her disposal may end up spending more time on the study than he/she had desired if a mathematical technique is used.

This is not to say that we should be hesitant about using these techniques. Besides the problems listed above, the techniques are also characterized by accuracy, simplicity, and richness. Researchers have refined the methods such that they are valid and do an excellent job of measuring what is intended. In addition, subjects rarely have difficulty understanding what they are being asked to do. The task can be completed quickly; as a result, despite having to perform many iterations, it usually does not become repetitive and boring. Finally, the composite data set can be very revealing, especially with the individualized regression approach. If cluster analysis produces more groupings than the researcher had anticipated, for example, the researcher may have some potentially interesting findings beyond his/her original hypothesis. The problems with social value measures are administrative rather than conceptual in nature, and administrative problems can often be overcome by collaboration with other researchers, extensions of the study's completion date, and so on.

Measures of Other Traits

There are some individual personality traits that are thought by many researchers to be related to social values. In this section, we want to describe what these traits are, as well as some of the more popular methods for assessing these traits.

Trust Scale

Cooperation is known to be related to trust (e.g., Alcock & Mansell, 1977; Deutsch, 1960b; Fox & Guyer, 1977; Messick *et al.*, 1983; see also Pruitt & Kimmel, 1977, and Wrightsman, 1991), and many researchers have attempted to develop a scale for assessing trust. An

TABLE 5.4 Yamagishi's (1986a) Trust Scale

1. Most people tell a lie when they can benefit by doing so.
2. Those devoted to unselfish causes are often exploited by others.
3. Some people do not cooperate because they pursue only their own short-term self-interest. Thus, things that can be done well if people cooperate often fail because of these people.
4. Most people are basically honest.
5. There will be more people who will not work if the social security system is developed further.

---

early such scale, the Philosophies of Human Nature Scale, was developed by Wrightsman (1966). More recently, Yamagishi (1986a) has developed a questionnaire (which is actually quite similar to Wrightsman's instrument) designed to measure degree of interpersonal trust. According to Yamagishi, trust is assumed to be continuous, ranging from high to low, and someone with high trust should be equivalent to a Cooperator, and someone with low trust equivalent to a Competitor or Individualist.

The Trust scale is a simple five-question form, shown in Table 5.4. These five questions were culled from a larger pool of questions developed by Yamagishi and Sato (1986). Subjects are asked to respond to each question by indicating the extent to which they agree with the statement on a five-point scale: "1" corresponds to complete agreement with the statement, on up to "5" corresponding to complete disagreement. Each subject's responses are then summed. For all statements but the fourth, the subject receives an amount of points equal to their response's position on the scale (e.g., a response of "3" to the second statement earns three points); the fourth statement is reverse-scored (e.g., a response of "1" earns five points). The points are then totalled, and the sum is assumed to reflect the degree of generalized trust the person has. The larger the total is, the more trusting the person is assumed to be.

Since trust and cooperation are believed to be related, we should see the frequency of cooperative behaviors increase as Trust scores increase. Using a public goods paradigm, Yamagishi (1986a) did in fact observe this relation. High-Trust subjects contributed on average about 56 percent of their total endowments toward provision of the public good, while Low-Trust subjects gave only about 33 percent of their endowments.

TABLE 5.5 Sample Items from Swap & Rubin's Interpersonal Orientation Scale

*I would rather think about a personal problem by myself than discuss it with others.

*Under no circumstances would I buy something I suspected had been stolen.

Sometimes the most considerate thing one person can do for another is to hide the truth.

*I am reluctant to talk about my personal life with people I do not know well.

It's important for me to work with people with whom I get along well, even if that means I get less done.

Note: Items with an asterisk (*) are reverse-scored.

Interpersonal Orientation

Another trait that has been related to cooperative and competitive behavior is Interpersonal Orientation (IO) (Rubin & Brown, 1975; Swap & Rubin, 1983). A person who is "high-IO" is concerned primarily with the relationship itself, that is, the actions and outcomes of the other person. A high-IO person is attuned to such things as reciprocity, equity, and orientation of the other person. (Note that no reference is made to *how* a high-IO responds to these factors; as such, Cooperators and Competitors are both considered high-IO, because both respond, albeit in different ways.) By contrast, a "low-IO" person cares only about his/her own gain. This person is driven solely to achieve the best personal outcome, regardless of how the other person fares, and will do whatever is necessary to realize this outcome. Low-IO is comparable to Individualism.

Interpersonal orientation is determined by using a questionnaire developed by Swap and Rubin (1983). The scale consists of 29 statements for which the subject must indicate his/her degree of agreement. Some sample items are shown in Table 5.5. As with the Trust scale, a five-point scale is used, with 1 = strongly disagree and 5 = strongly agree. Each response is scored by assigning a number of points corresponding to the person's scale position for that statement. Some statements are reverse-scored. After all responses have been scored, the values are summed, and this total reflects the person's degree of interpersonal orientation. A high score indicates that the person is high-IO; a low score, low-IO. Through a number of studies, Swap and Rubin have established that the scale is very reliable.

This conception of social values is somewhat different from the other approaches because it implies that specific response patterns will not necessarily be consistent across time. If the low-IO person can achieve the best personal outcomes by cooperating in one social relation and competing in a different relationship, this is exactly how he/she will respond. Similarly, a high-IO person might make competitive choices in a situation where he/she usually cooperates simply because the other person has violated a reciprocity norm. Thus, mere observation of a person's pattern of choices would not necessarily allow us to make accurate inferences regarding his/her motivational orientation.

Pull Scores

A final trait we want to consider is based on the notion of ''ingroups'' that we touched upon in Chapter 2. Henri Tajfel and his associates (e.g., Tajfel, Billig, Bundy, & Flament, 1971; Turner, 1978; Turner, Brown, & Tajfel, 1979) have argued that how one interacts with others is related to perceptions of the other person as an outgroup member. If one's general beliefs about outgroup members are negative, the resultant interaction with the person should be selfish (competitive or individualistic). In contrast, positive beliefs about outgroups should produce more congenial interactions (cooperation).

Tajfel and associates proposed matrices to determine what they refer to as ''pull scores.'' Originally conceived of as a measure of favoritism, it has been suggested that the scores may also reflect the extent to which a person is cooperative, competitive, or individualistic (Bornstein, Crum, Wittenbraker, Harring, Insko, & Thibaut, 1983). Sample matrices are shown in Table 5.6. The procedure is based on a paradigm in which the subject and one other person are to receive some resource (usually money), and the subject is asked to decide how the resource should be allocated to him/herself and the other person. To determine the ''pull'' of a particular social value, the subject simply chooses his/her most-preferred column from each of the two matrices. The choices are then scored using the scale shown underneath each matrix (the subject does not see this scale when making choices), and the two scores are subtracted from each other (matrix 1 – matrix 2). The

TABLE 5.6 Matrices for Determining Cooperative "Pull"

Matrix 1

Own	19	18	17	16	15	14	13	12	11	10	9	8	7
Other	1	3	5	7	9	11	13	15	17	19	21	23	25
Score	0	1	2	3	4	5	6	7	8	9	10	11	12

Matrix 2

Other	19	18	17	16	15	14	13	12	11	10	9	8	7
Own	1	3	5	7	9	11	13	15	17	19	21	23	25
Score	12	11	10	9	8	7	6	5	4	3	2	1	0

size of the difference is taken to indicate the relative strength of the particular motive; the larger the difference, the stronger the motive is assumed to be. The maximum possible pull, obviously, is $12 - 0 = 12$.

To illustrate, let's calculate some pull scores using the matrices in Table 5.6. These matrices would be used to determine the pull of cooperation, because extreme Competitors and Individualists would prefer the same columns ($19 - 1$ and $7 - 25$) and thus cannot be distinguished. Let's assume that our subject prefers the combination "16 to self, 7 to other" in the top matrix, and "8 to other, 23 to self" in the bottom. The $16 - 7$ choice earns three points and the $8 - 23$ choice one point, according to our scales. This results in a "pull" of 2. This person would seem to be basically noncooperative, though a small degree of cooperativeness does exist. By contrast, a person who prefers 10–19 and 9–21 would have a pull of $9 - 2 = 7$, and this person is quite cooperative.

Problems with Measures of Traits

The primary concern involving use of trait measures is that very little research has been done regarding their role in social dilemma behavior. Outside of Yamagishi's work on public goods, there has been little attempt to quantify trust and use it to predict dilemma behavior. There has been no research that we are aware of involving social dilemmas and either interpersonal orientation or pull scores. Researchers interested in whether we are predisposed to a particular course of action in social dilemmas would do well to investigate these traits.

Research on Social Values

As we have just seen, a question of major interest to researchers involves how we can accurately assess a person's social value. It is also of interest to determine how these values are related to individual behavior. Does one's social value orientation affect how one behaves in interpersonal settings? In this section, we shall look at some research that attempts to answer this question.

Intergame Stability

The original research on social values was conducted within a prisoner's dilemma game paradigm, that is, social values were used to predict choice behavior in the PDG. A logical question to ask is, how predictive are social values in other types of interpersonal situations? If values are predictive only of PDG behavior, then the topic may not be worthy of further research attention.

Many studies that have addressed the cross-situational stability of social values have used variants of the PDG. All of the studies we will discuss in this section assessed social values with the DPD technique. McClintock and Liebrand (1988) studied three such variants: Chicken, Leader, and Trust. Table 5.7 presents all three types of games. In the Chicken game, the worst outcome for both parties is in the "DD" cell; however, the best individual outcomes also requires a person to choose "D." Hence players end up in the DD cell almost immediately. The dilemma facing each player is, "Should I chicken out and switch to C, thus giving the opponent the best payoff, or hold on and hope he/she switches first?" We will discuss Chicken in much greater detail in Chapter 6. The next game is called the "Leader" game because both players will gain when one person "takes the lead" and switches away from mutual cooperation or defection. If there is mutual defection, however, the leader will increase the other person's payoff more than his/her own payoff, a situation which Competitors should find aversive. The Trust game is considered to be a trivial game, because it is obvious what each person should do: cooperate on the first trial and never switch. However, a competitor might find the (3,1) combination more attractive than (4,4), and as such may make some competitive choices in this game. McClintock and Liebrand did in fact find that choice behavior varied by value orientation in each of the three games. Cooperators made significantly more cooperative choices than either Individualists or Competitors, regardless of the game being played.

TABLE 5.7 Leader, Trust, and Chicken Games

Chicken	C	D		Leader	C	D
C	30,30	20,40		C	20,20	30,40
D	40,20	10,10		D	40,30	10,10

Trust	C	D
C	40,40	10,30
D	30,10	20,20

Liebrand, Wilke, Vogel, and Wolters (1986) also found significant differences between Cooperators and Competitors in the Chicken game. However, they found no differences in the Trust game.

Social values have also been investigated with a social trap paradigm. Liebrand (1984) examined the behaviors of Cooperators, Competitors, Individualists, and Altruists in a type of social trap called the Sequence Dilemma. A sequence dilemma is a game that combines the PDG and the resource dilemma. Each subject's goal is to obtain a requested amount of money from a resource pool. If total requests are less than the pool size, all persons receive their requests; if total requests exceed pool size, all receive zero. The sequence dilemma differs from the resource dilemma in that subjects make not one but five requests before the good is or is not provided. On the first trial, each person makes a request. On trials 2–5, the subjects are told what the total request was on the previous trial before they make their decision. Requests accumulate; thus, subjects can monitor the progress of their group and modify their subsequent requests accordingly.

Liebrand found social values to be very predictive in the sequence dilemma. On average, Competitors requested the most money on each trial, Cooperators and Altruists the least. (Individualists were intermediate.) However, social values did not predict how individuals would adapt their behavior over time. The requests of Individualists and Cooperators were consistent over trials, while Altruists and Competitors *increased* their requests as the game progressed. Liebrand and van Run (1985) demonstrated that these results are not culture-specific by showing that social values are predictive of Sequence Dilemma behavior in both the Netherlands and United States.

Kramer, McClintock, and Messick (1986) studied the predictive ability of social values in a standard resource dilemma situation. They classified people as either cooperators or noncooperators, and found that cooperators made increasingly smaller harvests as pool size shrank. By contrast, noncooperators did not significantly alter their harvesting behavior. Taken together, the studies of Liebrand and Kramer *et al.* would seem to indicate that social values have some predictive ability in social trap-type situations.

Beliefs

Many studies have been conducted to determine how one's social value orientation affects one's perceptions of others. Recall from Chapter 2 our discussion of Kelley and Stahelski's (1970a) "triangle hypothesis" of attributions in the PDG. Briefly, Kelley and Stahelski argued that competitors expect others to be competitive, while cooperators expect others to be more heterogeneous in orientation. Quite a few studies have supported their original assertion (e.g., Maki & McClintock, 1983; Maki, Thorngate, & McClintock, 1979; McClintock & Liebrand, 1988; Schlenker & Goldman, 1978). However, many studies have failed to demonstrate it (e.g., Dawes, MacTavish, & Shaklee, 1977; Kuhlman & Wimberley, 1976; Liebrand, 1984; Messe & Sivacek, 1979; Schulz, 1986). These latter studies showed a strong egocentric prediction bias: Both cooperators and competitors expect that others will act as they do. Thus the question of how one's value orientation relates to expectations about others is still unsettled.

Liebrand and colleagues have demonstrated that the very concept of "cooperation" is perceived differently by cooperators and noncooperators. For example, van Lange, Liebrand, and Kuhlman, (1990) and van Lange & Liebrand (1991a) found that Cooperators consider others who cooperate to be intelligent, and Noncooperators to be unintelligent, weak, and ignorant. Perhaps not surprisingly, Noncooperators demonstrated exactly the reverse pattern of perceptions. For them, other noncooperators are smart, cooperators are not. Both groups of people, however, agreed that cooperators are generally more concerned about the welfare of others than are noncooperators.

Perhaps the most interesting set of findings to emerge from this research revolves around how people define mixed-motive interaction. Liebrand, Jansen, Rijken, and Suhre, 1986 and McClintock & Liebrand, 1988 found that Cooperators consider the question of what to do in a socially interdependent situation to be one of morality. One should cooperate because it is "good" and "correct." By contrast, noncooperators think about cooperation in terms of power or "might." To the noncooperator, cooperation is a sign of weakness and capitulation, while defection shows strength and control. Thus, cooperators act as they do because they believe it to be the morally right response, and noncooperators defect in order to demonstrate that they have might. This "might versus morality" issue has spurred subsequent research. For example, van Lange and Liebrand (1991b) found that Noncooperators would not exploit an opponent whom they considered to be truly and completely moral (e.g., a priest). Studies by other researchers have strongly supported the notion that Cooperators view dilemma behavior as a question of morality; however, these same studies find little evidence that Noncooperators think in terms of power (Beggan, Messick, & Allison, 1988; Sattler & Kerr, 1991). The driving force behind a Cooperator's actions thus seems to be fairly clear. However, more work is necessary for us to establish why Noncooperators act as they do.

Changing Behavior

Finally, some investigators have asked whether basic value-driven behavior can be changed or altered by external factors. McNeel (1973) studied Individualists and Competitors to see if their behavior could be made more cooperative. McNeel tested the effects of two factors: the strategy of the other person and the availability of a standard of comparison. He hypothesized that Individualists, when playing against a tit-for-tat type of strategy, would learn that personal gain (when playing TFT) can best be maximized by cooperating. (Kahn, Hottes, & Davis, 1971, offered a similar hypothesis.) He further hypothesized that Individualists will become more cooperative when they discover that their competitive choices have produced a below-average point total. Neither the strategy of the other person nor standard of comparison was expected to affect the choices of Competitors.

To test these hypotheses, McNeel first determined social values with the DPD method. Individualists and Competitors then participated in a two-person PDG. For half of the subjects, the "other" was actually a simulated TFT; the rest served as control subjects. Half of the subjects also received (bogus) trial-by-trial information indicating that their point total was lower than that of the average subject; the rest received no such information. Consistent with expectations, McNeel found that Individualists who played against the TFT strategy had significantly higher frequencies of cooperative response than the respective control group. In fact, 80 percent of the Individualists who played against TFT eventually became purely cooperative. In contrast, Competitors were unaffected by strategy; their rates of cooperative response remained very low (less than 20 percent). With regard to the effects of "standard of comparison," Individualists presented with such a standard became cooperative more quickly than the control. The standard had no effect on Competitors. It seems, then, that Individualists will become cooperative if they believe that competition is producing a suboptimal personal outcome. Competitors seem to be insensitive to such information.

Liebrand, Wilke *et al.* (1986) looked at how information about the choices of others affects future behavior. Social values were determined via the DPD method. Subjects then played an eight-person PDG, Chicken, or Trust game for money. After the third trial, subjects received bogus feedback about the others' choices. Half of the subjects were told that the majority of other group members had chosen cooperatively on each trial; the other half were told the majority had chosen competitively. After receiving this feedback, five more trials of the games were conducted.

Liebrand and colleagues' results are shown in Table 5.8. You can see that frequency of cooperation was strongly affected by the structure of the game. Majority-C feedback had little effect on behavior, regardless of the structure of the game. Competitors in the PDG game cooperated more frequently after receiving the information, but Cooperators did not change at all. Similarly, majority-D information had little effect on Cooperators; in fact, it actually *increased* cooperation in the Chicken game. However, such information caused Competitors to significantly decrease their rate of cooperative response in the PDG and Trust games.

Liebrand and colleagues explained these results by arguing that competition is generally a socially unacceptable behavior, and a person who is competitive will show restraint because of this unacceptability. (This would explain why the pre-feedback cooperation rate is higher than usually observed for Competitors.) Learning that

TABLE 5.8 Results of the Liebrand, Wilke, Vogel, and Wolters
(1986) Study

		Frequency of Cooperation		
Orientation	Condition	PDG	Chicken	Trust
Cooperation	Before fdbk	.69	.73	.96
	After Maj-D	.53	.87	.94
	After Maj-C	.74	.70	.96
Competition	Before fdbk	.32	.59	.96
	After Maj-D	.11	.51	.74
	After Maj-C	.48	.63	.92

most others are cooperative further inhibits competitive tendencies;
however, discovering that most other people are competitive serves
to remove the stigma from competition and encourages the competitor to act as he/she pleases. Thus, in real-world situations one must
be careful about how choice feedback is presented, especially if one
is dealing with Competitors.

Where Do Values Come From?

We have argued that social values are part of one's personality, and
we have seen that there are systematic differences in the behavior of
Cooperators and Competitors in different types of social dilemma
games. Further, it is not clear (though the number of studies is
small) how easy it is to increase the frequency of cooperation
among Competitors. Throughout this book, we have seen that in social dilemmas, competition is a strategy that is suboptimal in the
long run. There are many instances in which it is desirable to minimize the number of Competitors in society (e.g., support of charitable organizations). What can we do if we cannot change the
behavior of Competitors?

One approach to this problem involves intervention at an early
age. If we knew how and when social values come about, we could
go to children for whom a value had not yet developed and teach
them the value of cooperation. This is an easy and cost-effective
intervention that can be implemented by parents and schools. The
question we first need to answer, though, is, "When and how do
social values develop?"

TABLE 5.9 A Maximizing Difference Game

	C	D
C	6,6	0,5
D	5,0	0,0

Charles McClintock is one of the leading researchers in the area of social values. We have already discussed some of his and his colleagues' work. He has also extensively investigated the development of social values in children. Perhaps the first study to examine this issue was conducted by McClintock and Nuttin (1969). They studied 336 second, fourth, and sixth grade children from America and Belgium. The children played a variant of the PDG called a Maximizing Difference Game (MDG) (McClintock & McNeel, 1966). A sample MDG is shown in Table 5.9. Because a cooperative choice maximizes both own and joint gain, the only person for whom defection should be attractive is the Competitor. The game was put into a form which children could easily understand: The letters "C" and "D" were replaced with buttons that the child could press in order to register a choice. Each cell contained a light that, when lit, indicated what the payoff was. Pairs of children (same grade, same nationality) played the game. Half of the children received information about only their own payoff; the other half learned both own and other's payoffs.

McClintock and Nuttin obtained some very interesting results, shown in Table 5.10. Overall, the Belgian children were significantly less competitive than their American counterparts (.56 vs. .65). For each culture, competition increased with grade (.48, .60, to .73). But note that American children made a sharp increase from second to fourth grade, while Belgians made a large jump from fourth to sixth grade. Also note that, by sixth grade, competitiveness was completely consistent (equal) across cultures (.73 each).

Information also seemed to have an effect: Children who knew both payoffs were more competitive than those who knew only their own. It should be stated that, while the overall rate for second graders was almost 50–50, McClintock and Nuttin found no evidence that those children were responding randomly. They did discover that as grade increased, children became increasingly

TABLE 5.10 Mean Percentage of Competitive Responses: McClintock & Nuttin Study

	American	Belgian	Mean
2nd grade	.54	.43	.48
4th grade	.67	.53	.60
6th grade	.73	.73	.73
Mean	.65	.56	

sensitive to exploitation; for example, the Belgian sixth graders made a competitive choice 87 percent of the time if they had been exploited on the previous trial.

Toda, Shinotsuka, McClintock, and Stech (1978) replicated these findings almost exactly with Greek and Japanese students. Each of these two cultures demonstrated a pattern similar to that of McClintock and Nuttin's American students: a large increase in competitiveness from the second to fourth grade, followed by a small increase from fourth to sixth grade. Interestingly, the Japanese and Greek second graders competed with almost exactly the same frequency as American students (around .50), but sixth graders were more competitive than their American counterparts (around .80 for each culture).

Finally, McClintock (1974) was able to replicate almost all of these findings in a study comparing American and Mexican-American children. As in the Belgian study, Mexican-American children were significantly less competitive than American children, though both cultures showed the familiar increase in competitiveness with grade. Overall competition rates were remarkably consistent; for example, American sixth graders responded competitively almost 75 percent of the time, Mexican-American nearly 65 percent. The Mexican-American children, however, showed a steady increase in competitiveness, rather than the large increase-small increase pattern observed in the Japanese, Greek, and American cultures. In a related series of studies, Madsen and colleagues (Kagan & Madsen, 1971, 1972; Knight & Kagan, 1977; Madsen, 1971; Madsen & Shapira, 1970) also showed that Mexican-American children, while becoming increasingly competitive with age, are overall less competitive than American children.

TABLE 5.11 Summary of McClintock's Cross-Cultural Studies

	Frequency of Competition in Grade		
Nationality	2nd	4th	6th
American	.54	.67	.73
Belgian	.43	.53	.73
Mexican-American	.53	.58	.64
Japanese	.49	.70	.78
Greek	.48	.72	.80

The results of McClintock and colleagues' cross-cultural studies are summarized in Table 5.11. The obvious conclusion from these studies is that competitiveness develops over time in children. Further, this phenomenon is more or less universal, having been demonstrated in a wide variety of cultures. Note, however, that even second graders (about seven or eight years old in America) are already showing some preference for competition. Is there a time when children do *not* think in competitive terms?

McClintock addressed this issue by studying American children from nursery school through second grade (McClintock & Moskowitz, 1976; McClintock, Moskowitz, & McClintock, 1977; see also McClintock & Keil, 1983). The children attempted to win playing DPDs that were cooperative, competitive, or individualistic. (The studies were within-subjects; that is, all children played all three game variants.) The very youngest of these children (3–4 years old) showed purely egoistic behavior regardless of the structure of the outcome matrix. That is, the children preferred to maximize own short-term gain, even if it was in their long-term best interest not to do so. (McClintock and Keil, 1983, suggest that children act this way because they cannot yet conceive of concepts like fairness.) McClintock and colleagues found that, around the age of 4 1/2, the children began to learn and apply the concept of competition and to think of long-term versus short-term gains; the children seemed to understand cooperation at about the age of 6 or 7. (Similar results were obtained by Stingle & Cook, 1985.)

Two explanations have been offered for this finding. McClintock and Keil (1983) argued that cooperation and competition are socialized into the child, and that competition (at least in the cultures studied) is taught before cooperation, though at differing points in the child's development; recall that Belgian children did not show large increases in competition until after the fourth grade. (It would be interesting to know how behavior would be affected if this pattern of socialization were reversed.) Knight, Dubro, and Chao (1985) suggested that the learning of competition and cooperation is a function of the development of the child's information-processing capabilities. They argued that competition is a less complex concept than cooperation, and as such is more easily learned. Thus, children learn competition before cooperation simply because their mental capabilities cannot accommodate learning them in the reverse order.

Sex Differences

It is common in studies of the development of social values to observe a difference in behavior between boys and girls. Unfortunately, the differences have been inconsistent. Some studies have found boys to be more competitive than girls (e.g., Fitzgerald & Frankie, 1982; Kagan & Madsen, 1972; Madsen & Shapira, 1970; McClintock & Moskowitz, 1976), while other studies show girls are more competitive than boys (e.g., Sampson & Kardush, 1965; Tedeschi, Hiester, & Gahagan, 1969). In reviewing these studies, Knight and Kagan (1981) identified a problem consistent to all of the experiments: Individualism had been confounded with either cooperation or competition. They argued that the observed sex differences were purely a function of individualism: boys and girls differ not in terms of their competitiveness, but in terms of their individualism. We have seen that very young children are strongly individualistic (McClintock & Moskowitz, 1976; McClintock, Moskowitz, & McClintock, 1977). Perhaps this egotistical streak persists into late childhood.

Some evidence for this argument was first documented by Knight, Kagan, and Buriel (1981). They found that, when presented as a distinct option, individualism was very popular among American children. A more rigorous test was provided by Knight and Kagan (1981). They developed a motivational orientation assessment technique with three conditions: 1) Individualism, cooperation, and competition were distinctly different options; 2) Individualism and cooperation were confounded; and 3) Individualism and competition were confounded. Table 5.12 shows a sample choice matrix from each condition. Knight and Kagan hypothesized that, in Condition 1, more girls than boys would choose option B (the individualistic choice); in Condition 2, more girls than boys would choose

TABLE 5.12 Sample of Knight & Kagan's (1981) Technique

Condition 1: Individualism Distinct Choice

Payoff to	A	B	C
Self	5	6	5
Peer	5	3	1

Condition 2: Individualism-Cooperation Confounded Choice

Payoff to	A	B	C
Self	5	4	4
Peer	5	3	1

Condition 3: Individualism-Competition Confounded Choice

Payoff to	A	B	C
Self	5	5	6
Peer	5	3	1

Option A (the individualistic and cooperative choice); and in Condition 3, more girls than boys would choose Option C (the individualistic and competitive choice).

At first glance, Knight and Kagan's prediction might seem strange to you (or, at least to American readers). The stereotypical American girl is perceived by many to be very cooperative, while boys are taught to be tough and competitive. But Knight and Kagan argue that above all, ours is an individualistic culture; we celebrate the "rugged individualist" and "self-made" individual. This value is passed along to our children. However, Knight and Kagan argue that deviance from social norms is tolerated more in boys than in girls. We look upon the eccentric man more favorably than on the eccentric woman. The corollary of this is that girls will adhere more strictly to cultural norms than will boys. Since one of our basic norms is individualism, it follows that girls will be more individualistic than boys. In support of their argument, it should be noted that earlier work in cultures that are not considered individualistic (Mexican, Korean, American Indian) found no differences in individualism between boys and girls (Madsen & Shapira, 1970; Madsen & Yi, 1975; Miller & Thomas, 1972).

In fact, Knight and Kagan's predictions were confirmed. In Condition 1, girls were more individualistic than boys, and there were no sex differences regarding cooperation-competition; in Condition 2, girls were more cooperative than boys; and in Condition 3, girls were more competitive than boys. This suggests that the confusing sex differences documented in earlier studies were probably a function of the individualism confound. (Knight & Chao, 1989, obtained similar results.)

Summary

Social values, assumed to be part of one's personality, can exert a strong influence on one's behavior in an interpersonal situation. Many different techniques exist to assess a person's value orientation. In addition, some other personality traits are thought to be related to dilemma behavior. However, research that firmly establishes this link is scant.

Social values have been found to be consistent over a wide variety of PDG-type games as well as some social traps. Though studies are few, there seems to be little that can be done to induce Competitors to become more cooperative.

A large area of research has addressed the development of social values in children. The progress with which values develop seems consistent over a wide variety of cultures. Any differences in sex seems to be on Individualism.

6

Social Dilemmas and Interdisciplinary Issues

Social dilemma research is of interest to a variety of scientists besides psychologists, primarily because social dilemmas are adaptable to many situations. Many global conflicts have been described as being a type of prisoner's dilemma (e.g., Brams & Kilgour, 1988; Lumsden, 1973). Students of biological science also find the PDG attractive. In particular, evolutionary biologists are interested in the question of if and how animals learn the principle of reciprocity. Research has been conducted on animals as diverse as bats, fish, monkeys, and birds (Axelrod & Dion, 1988). In fact, the application of social dilemma principles to issues that are not strictly psychological is relatively common.

Perhaps the best evidence of PDG's widespread popularity lies in one of the major scientific journals that publishes such research. If you have glanced at this book's reference section, you may have noticed that many of the studies we have cited were published in the *Journal of Conflict Resolution*. This journal emphasizes theory and research on the causes and resolution of conflict and the promotion of cooperation at the interpersonal as well as the global level, a major approach in which the social dilemma paradigm is used. The journal is truly interdisciplinary; the editorial board consists of economists, political scientists, sociologists, anthropologists, and mathematicians, as well as psychologists. To further illustrate, consider some of the individuals who appear frequently in this text. Robert Axelrod, Steven Brams, John Orbell, and Alphons van de Kragt are political scientists; Anatol Rapoport is a mathematician; Gerald Marwell, Henry Hamburger and Toshio Yamagishi are sociologists; and Thomas Schelling and Vernon Smith are economists.

In this chapter, we shall examine work in political science, finance, and biology. We shall examine how such research is conducted, and present some of the major research findings.

Political Science

Researchers interested in political issues often rely on a prisoner's dilemma framework to study and theorize about such issues. Now we want to look at this modelling in more detail, with special attention paid to the arms race.

The Arms Race

Before the breakup of the Soviet Union, considerable attention was focused on the continual buildup of the Soviet and American arsenals. Today, the nuclear threat to America is greatly diminished. However, analysis of the 40-year "arms race" is still instructive, if for no other reason than to offer lessons for future international conflict.

Gaming and the Arms Race: History

Comparison of the arms race to a social dilemma has its roots in the early 1960s, when a series of books by Charles Osgood (1962), Anatol Rapoport (1960; 1964; Rapoport & Chammah, 1965), and Thomas Schelling (1960) argued that the then-young race to acquire nuclear weapons could easily be described as a prisoner's

TABLE 6.1 A Model of the Arms Race

		Soviet Union	
		Disarm	*Arm*
United States	Disarm	3, 3	1, 4
	Arm	4, 1	2, 2

dilemma. This depiction of the arms race as a prisoner's dilemma is shown in Table 6.1. The numbers in each cell refer to utility of outcomes, with 4 being the most-preferred outcome, 1 the least-preferred. Note that the conditions of the PDG are satisfied: $T > R > P > S$ ($4 > 3 > 2 > 1$) and $2R > T + S$ ($3 + 3 > 4 + 1$). In this game, each country has a choice between continued armament or disarmament. Arming dominates disarming, because no matter what the other country does, it is better to arm: If the Soviets arm, America should also arm in order to "keep up;" if the Soviets disarm, America can gain a missile advantage by continuing to arm. The dilemma lies in the cost of the missiles. Mutual armament (the competitive choice) is much more expensive than mutual disarmament (the cooperative choice). Thus, both countries would like to move from competition to cooperation, but neither is willing to risk a missile disadvantage to do so.

These works immediately spurred attempts to systematically study the arms race in game-theoretic terms. An extensive series of experimental studies was undertaken by Pilisuk and colleagues (Pilisuk, Potter, Rapoport, & Winter, 1965; Pilisuk & Rapoport, 1964; Pilisuk & Skolnick, 1968; Pilisuk, Winter, Chapman, & Haas, 1967; see also Pilisuk, 1984). In these studies, each subject was given a stock of missiles to manage. The task was to decide how many missiles to maintain, and how many to convert to factories (done by scrapping a missile and using the money to build a factory). Pilisuk used a modified two-person prisoner's dilemma, altered in such a way that each subject had not two but 21 different choices, ranging from complete armament to complete disarmament. Further, in the later studies (Pilisuk *et al.,* 1967; Pilisuk & Skolnick, 1968) subjects had the opportunity to "inspect" their opponent's total missile stock.

Pilisuk and colleagues found that subjects' behavior in these modified arms games was very similar to that in a traditional prisoner's dilemma: The use of a tit-for-tat-like strategy (i.e., maintaining a missile stock equal to or less than the size of one's opponent's stock) elicited greater cooperation than any other strategy. Curiously, subjects in these conditions often could not verbalize what strategy the opponent was using. The work of Pilisuk and colleagues was thus very important in establishing the feasibility of using social dilemma paradigms to simulate the arms race. Many other studies have since bolstered and expanded on Pilisuk's basic work (e.g., Brams, 1975; Brams, David, & Straffin, 1979; Guyer, Fox, & Hamburger, 1973; Jervis, 1978; Lindskold, 1978; Miller & Holmes, 1975; Shubik, 1968, 1970; Snyder, 1971; Snyder & Diesing, 1977).

What Type of Game?

As a result of this work, most political scientists assume that arms races can be modeled as some form of game (though Snidal (1985b) has commented that PDG-type games are often misused by political scientists). The question now seems to be, "what type of game is the most appropriate model?" Most feel that the standard prisoner's dilemma is best (Brams, 1985); in fact, Downs, Rocke, and Siverson (1985) present some examples of actual arms conflicts that seem to have had a PDG structure. However, many researchers believe that some variant of the PDG is more realistic (e.g., Anderton, 1989; Shubik, 1970; Snyder, 1971; Taylor, 1987; Wagner, 1983). Some criticisms of the PDG as a political model that are generally offered are: a) the game is too simplistic because it restricts choices to only two options; b) political interactions unfold over a much longer period of time than even iterated games can simulate; c) real-world political choices are not made simultaneously, but rather sequentially; and d) the required payoff ordering of T > R > P > S is often inaccurate. Consequently, many researchers have attempted to devise games that more accurately reflect the intricacies of such conflicts. We will now summarize some of those alternate games.

Chicken

Many political scientists believe that a simple reordering of the PDG payoffs is sufficient to capture the nature of arms races. This reordering produces a variant of the PDG called CHICKEN. You will remember our discussion of Chicken games from Chapter 2; a Chicken payoff matrix appears in Table 6.2. A value of 4 indicates the most-preferred outcome; 1 represents the least-preferred outcome. Unlike the PDG, there is no dominant choice in Chicken. If your opponent cooperates, you should not; but if he/she does not

TABLE 6.2 Chicken

	Disarm	Arm
Disarm	3, 3	2, 4
Arm	4, 2	1, 1

cooperate, you should. Chicken has received considerable attention from political scientists (e.g., Brams, 1975; Hardin, 1983; Snyder & Diesing, 1977; Taylor, 1987).

It has been shown that cooperation is greater in Chicken than in the PDG, and that cooperation can be improved by worsening the outcome in the DD cell. In the political realm, it is assumed that the most-preferred outcome for either country is military superiority (achieved by arming while one's opponent disarms). The "chicken" is the country that first switches from arming to disarmament so as to avoid the worst outcome (war) and thus becomes inferior militarily.

Some scientists feel that global conflict is more accurately modeled with PDG variants other than Chicken. For example, in the *Deadlock game* (Downs *et al.*, 1985), the CC and DD cells of the PDG are reversed. Arming dominates disarming for both players. In the real world, this would correspond to actual conflict being more preferable than being seen as a "second-rate" military power, and as such, there exists no incentive to disarm. In the *Stag Hunt game* (Jervis, 1978; Oye, 1985) the *Reward* and *Temptation* values of the PDG are reversed. Thus, the most-preferred outcome is achieved through mutual cooperation. However, this game assumes that defection is "easier" than cooperation, and that the actors will opt for the easy solution rather than work hard to achieve their most-preferred outcome.

Chicken, Deadlock, and Stag Hunt models are somewhat popular. However, many theorists believe that modeling arms races with a PDG requires more than simply reordering preferences. We next want to look at some of these more fundamental alterations of the prisoner's dilemma.

The Security Dilemma

Jervis (1978) has proposed a PDG variant called the security dilemma. He argued that, in the real world, outcomes matrices may be *asymmetric,* and the payoffs for combinations of choices may not

TABLE 6.3 A Security Dilemma

a. Symmetric Payoffs

		Player 1	
		C	D
Player 2	C	"4," 4	"3," 3
	D	"3," 3	"3," 3

b. Asymmetric Payoffs

		Player 1	
		C	D
Player 2	C	"3," 4	"4," 3
	D	"4," 3	"4," 3

be the same for each player. Further, in the real world it is very difficult (if not impossible) to know exactly what the other party's payoff matrix looks like; in most instances, we can only make an informed guess. For example, we might suppose that an enemy's utility for losing thousands of lives is highly negative, but we have no way of knowing this for sure; perhaps the leader wants to be a martyr. This presents an interesting dilemma: How can we maximize our personal payoff if we do not know our opponent's preferred outcomes?

Table 6.3 presents some simple security dilemma matrices. Again, the cell entries refer to preferences, with 4 being most-preferred, and choices are assumed to be sequential rather than simultaneous. (We have put Player 2's payoffs in quotation marks to indicate that these values are assumed by, rather than known to, Player 1.) Table 6.3a depicts a situation in which Player 1 assumes Player 2's preferences are the same as his/her own. In other words, Player 1 believes the payoffs to be symmetric. Cooperation is the weakly dominant choice for Player 1, and is believed to be the same for Player 2. Thus, Player 1 should cooperate regardless of whether he/she chooses first or second.

Table 6.3b illustrates an assumption of asymmetric payoffs. In this instance, Player 1 is assuming that Player 2's payoff structure is different from his/her own. Cooperation is still the weakly dominant choice for Player 1, but competition is believed to be weakly dominant for Player 2. Now, it is not clear what choice Player 1 should make, and in fact, sequence makes an important difference: Whoever chooses second can completely determine the outcome of the first-chooser.

Jervis (see also Wagner, 1983) has argued that the solution to this dilemma lies in the range of choices one has. He suggests that, in the real world, each player will have a collection of *intermediate choices* available. In this sense, the C and D choices represent extreme endpoints of a response continuum. For example, in the real world there may exist a third alternative *C'* that is not as purely cooperative as C, but yet may produce an outcome better than that which the competitive choice produces. Acceptance of an outcome that is not one's most-preferred is known as "satisficing" (Simon, 1957).

To illustrate, let's continue with our example of going to war. We will define the purely cooperative (C) choice as complete pacificism, and the purely competitive (D) choice as an all-out attack. Let's assume that you do not want to go to war, but you believe that Player 2 is hostile and wants to fight. Thus, your payoff matrix resembles Table 6.3b. If you are pacificistic and choose C, then Player 2 will invade and capture your country. If you choose D and attack, then the resulting conflict will lead to a massive loss of your citizens' lives. What do you do? To solve this, let's introduce a third option, C', *an economic embargo*. Under this choice, you and your allies will refuse to send valuable resources to Player 2. This choice is cooperative in that no combat is involved, yet competitive in that Player 2 is being harmed in some way. The outcome to you is not the best (because you will lose income), but it is better than war. This resolution is very similar to the C-C choice combination in the prisoner's dilemma: Your personal outcome is not the most-preferred, but it is not your least-preferred either.

Kramer has recently studied a form of the Security Dilemma and how it affects decisions to allocate money. In his studies, subjects act the part of world leaders. A multi-trial game, each subject is given points at the start of every trial, and he/she must decide how many points to invest in security and/or domestic wealth. Investment in security allows the leader to build a strong military; investments in wealth are turned into real money that the subject receives at the end of the game. Each leader must also announce on every trial how much he/she is investing in security, though this announcement is nonbinding; it could easily be used as a bluff. When a total of 300 points have been invested in security, the leader has the option of "attacking" the opponent and stealing some of the opponent's points, which can then be invested in the leader's own economy. However, if the opponent's security account has more points, the invasion will be unsuccessful. Thus the dilemma: should one neglect wealth and build up security for an attack, hoping the opponent's security force is small, or pour one's points into domestic wealth and hope not to be attacked? An unsuccessful invasion would mean a small monetary payoff, because the wealth account would contain few points; however, weak security could leave one's large wealth account vulnerable to attack.

This version of the Security Dilemma is very new, so at this point we know little about individual behavior in this situation. Kramer and colleagues (Kramer, 1989; Kramer, Meyerson, & Davis, 1990) have learned that feedback that is comparative in form has strong effects on allocation decisions. Comparative feedback tells the subject how the state of his/her programs compares to the opponent (e.g., "Your opponent has built up more security than you have."). Kramer's studies indicate that subjects are sensitive to deficits and will attempt to rectify them by diverting points originally intended for the other program. Thus, a subject who learns that he/she has a deficit in wealth will decrease future allocations to security and increase allocations to wealth, and vice versa for a security deficit. Given the attractiveness of the paradigm, it is likely that we will learn much more about behavior in a security dilemma in the near future.

Coordination Games

Another game that is often used in the study of politics is the coordination game. The coordination game has been discussed by theorists for centuries (Gilbert, 1984), but it was first formalized by Schelling in 1960, and extended by Lewis (1969) and Snidal (1985a). The outcome matrix is shown in Table 6.4. Once again, the numbers refer to preference rankings, with 4 being the most-preferred outcome for a given player. (In the coordination game, a player's choice is not usually defined as being between

TABLE 6.4 A Coordination Game

		Player 2	
		A	B
Player 1	A	4, 3	2, 2
	B	1, 1	3, 4

a cooperative or competitive action, but simply between two alternate actions; hence, we shall call the options "A" and "B" rather than "C" and "D.") You will notice that it is similar in structure to the Leader game discussed in Chapter 5. In the coordination game, however, the emphasis is on *similarity of preferences*. Notice that the two most-preferred outcomes for each player are located in the A-A and B-B cells. In the coordination game, each player would rather have his/her choice match that of the other person. The dilemma, of course, is that if each player pursues his/her most-preferred outcome, Player 1 will choose A and Player 2 will choose B, and the result will be mismatched behaviors.

Coordination games are quite common in the real world (see Gordon & Pelkmans, 1979; Taylor, 1987). Snidal (1985a) gives as an example of the problem of different standards of measurement throughout the world. Define choice "A" as the Metric System, and choice "B" as the United States Weights and Measures System. This is obviously not a cooperative-competitive choice, as either system will do an acceptable job of assessment. Consider Player 1 to be Canada and Player 2 to be the United States. Each country must decide which standard of measurement to adopt. Because of their frequent interaction and common border, the countries would like the systems to be uniform. However, Canada most prefers the Metric System, the U.S. their own. Each country has pursued their own preferences; as a result, the countries are in the undesirable A-B cell. American travelers in Canada must cope with an unfamiliar system of kilometers and liters, and vice versa.

The coordination game suggests many interesting questions that appeal to the psychologist as well as the political scientist or economist. For example, players may have differing utilities for coordination itself, that is, one player may value coordination more than the other player. Regarding the measurement example, the United States' attitude toward uniformity may be that, while it would be nice, the country will not be too adversely affected by mismatched measurement systems. On the other hand, Canada, which is quite economically dependent on America, may desperately want coordinated systems of measurement. Canada would thus value coordination much more than would America. How would these differing utilities affect behavior? A related question involves influence. If one player strongly values coordination, how might he/she attempt to convince the other to feel likewise?

A key element in coordination is communication. We have seen repeatedly that interaction greatly increases cooperation rates, and if all else is equal, the participants in a coordination game should immediately reach a solution. But what if the participants cannot interact? Halpern (1986; see also Rubenstein, 1989) has posed an interesting scenario that addresses this question. Known as the "coordinated attack problem" the parable is as follows: Two battalions of an army are stationed on opposite hills, with the enemy in the center. The enemy is very strong, and a single battalion alone could not defeat it, but two battalions working together could win if they launch a surprise attack. This is what the battalions on the hills want to do. However, the enemy's location in between them precludes any overt communication, since any such messages can be intercepted. The battalions must interact by means of secret messenger. The general of the first battalion sends a messenger to the second with the message, "Attack at 0400 hours." But how does the general know the message got through? Suppose the messenger returns with an "OK" from the second general; how does the second general know the confirmation got through? Let the first general send the messenger back with a confirmation of the confirmation; how does the general know it was received? You can see that this would go on indefinitely (or at least until 0400 hours had passed). The interesting question is, at what point would each general simply assume that the other knew what to do? This is a question that has not yet received the attention of psychologists, but is well worth study.

Is One Game Adequate?

Finally, some political scientists feel that one single game cannot model all arms races (Downs & Rocke, 1987). For example, Russell Hardin (1983) identified seven different games, all of which he argued could accurately characterize the American-Soviet arms race alone. Schelling (1984) argued that any one of *sixteen* alternate PDG games could plausibly model an arms race. Still others argue that the basic game must be combined with mathematical choice functions (which are beyond the scope of this book to explain) to adequately capture the nature of the conflict (Isard & Anderton, 1985; Lichbach, 1989, 1990). Clearly, the debate over how best to model the arms race in game terms is not likely to subside soon.

The Perceptual Dilemma
Most experimental social dilemmas are *symmetric*; in other words, every person's payoff matrix is exactly alike. Further, in most games players have *complete information* about every other player's

payoff utilities because they are told that all matrices are the same. But what if this were not true? In a series of studies, Plous (1985, 1987, 1988) hypothesized that, at least in the American-Soviet arms race, this symmetry is *not* the case. Rather, each side holds false beliefs about the most-preferred outcomes of the other. He called this a "Perceptual Dilemma" and argued that it could be modeled as a two-person prisoner's dilemma.

To test these hypotheses, Plous (1985) first content-analyzed a number of public statements made by American and Soviet leaders from 1981 to 1984 regarding the arms race. He found considerable evidence to support his perceptual dilemma hypothesis. For example, regarding own most-preferred outcome, President Reagan was quoted (*New York Times,* 6/15/84) as saying, "We want more than anything else to join with [the Soviet Union] in reducing the number of weapons," and Soviet Secretary Chernenko said (*Pravda,* 4/9/84), "We have been and remain convinced advocates of halting the arms race and reversing it." Both of these comments would seem to indicate that, for each country, the highest outcome can be attained by mutual disarmament. Misperceptions were also evident in public comments. For example, Reagan argued (*New York Times,* 6/28/84), "For the Soviet leaders peace is not the real issue; rather, the issue is the attempt to spread their dominance using military power." Along the same lines, Soviet Secretary Andropov stated (*Pravda,* 1/13/84), "The main obstacle and the entire course of the Geneva talks is persuasive evidence of . . . attempts by the U.S. and its allies to achieve military superiority." Clearly, each leader is claiming that the other wants more than anything to assemble a massive, unparalleled arsenal.

Public statements, however, can often contain more rhetoric than belief. Maybe the preceding quotes were given more to encourage anti-Sovietism or anti-Americanism than to indicate what the leader truly believes. To check this, Plous contacted President Reagan, Secretary of Defense Weinberger, and members of the United States Senate and Soviet Politburo and asked them to rate, on a scale of −10 to +10, the desirability of mutual disarmament, mutual armament, unilateral disarmament by the Soviet Union, and unilateral disarmament by the United States. The politicians were asked not only to rate the four conditions, but also to rate the conditions as they believed the *other side* would.

Plous received responses from only the U.S. Senate. Thirty-two senators responded. The data are summarized in Table 6.5. The left entry in each cell represents the mean rank preference of the

TABLE 6.5 Results of Plous' (1985) Survey
of American Senators

		Soviet Union	
		Disarm	*Arm*
United States	Disarm	8.0, 5.9	–6.7, 7.0
	Arm	1.0, –7.3	–5.3, –0.9

From S. Plous, "Perceptual Illusions and Military Realities: The nuclear arms race" in
Journal of Conflict Resolution, 1985, Vol. 29, pp. 363–389. Copyright © 1985 Sage
Publications, Inc. Reprinted by permission of Sage Publications, Inc.

senators, whereas the right entry in each cell represents the Soviet's
rank preferences—*as perceived by the senators*. The table clearly
indicates a perceptual bias among the senators. Mutual disarmament
was strongly preferred by the Americans (8.0); however, they believed that the Soviets most desired unilateral disarmament by the
U.S. (7.0).

Based on the data in Table 6.5, Plous constructed the theoretical matrices shown in Table 6.6. Note that the game is not a
PDG, but is instead a "coordination game." As in Table 6.1, the
numbers refer to preference rankings, with 4 being most desirable.
Table 6.6a shows the true situation. Both countries would like more
than anything to disarm. If this is not possible, the next-best situation would be to have the enemy disarm while we arm. Tables 6.6b
and c show how, Plous argues, each country *believes* the other
would like the situation to be. Each country believes that the enemy's most-preferred outcome is unilateral disarmament, (e.g., disarm while the enemy does not). If this is not possible, each country
would like mutual disarmament. (Frei, 1986, has also commented on
misperceptions.)

Perceptual dilemmas, then, seem to occur in the real world.
What can be done about them? We saw in Chapter 2 that tit-for-tat
is effective in promoting cooperation in the prisoner's dilemma; is
there a similar cooperation-enhancing strategy in the perceptual dilemma? To provide an answer to this question, Plous (1987) compared two plausible strategies: Status Quo (SQ), in which one
simply matches the actions of the other person; and Disarmament
Initiatives (DI), in which one makes an initial series of unconditionally cooperative responses (ten trials in Plous' experiment) followed
by matching. Subjects competed in a 30-trial perceptual dilemma

TABLE 6.6 Misperceptions by Americans and Soviets

a. The True Situation

		Soviet Union	
		Disarm	*Arm*
United States	Disarm	4,4	1,3
	Arm	3,1	2,2

b. American Misperceptions about Soviets

		Soviet Union	
		Disarm	*Arm*
United States	Disarm	4,3	1,4
	Arm	3,1	2,2

c. Soviet Misperceptions about Americans

		Soviet Union	
		Disarm	*Arm*
United States	Disarm	3,4	1,3
	Arm	4,1	2,2

TABLE 6.7 An Experimental Perceptual Dilemma

		Other	
		C	*D*
You	C	8, 6	−7, 7
	D	1, −7	5, −1

using the matrix shown in Table 6.7. Half of the subjects played
against a preprogrammed "other" who played an SQ strategy and
the other half played against a DI strategy. The payoff values simulate the perceptions of the U.S. senators shown in Table 6.5.

Plous found the SQ and DI strategies to have very different
effects on behavior. At the outset, all subjects made a high frequency

of competitive (D) responses (more than 80 percent). However, by the end of the game, subjects playing against DI made competitive responses only 12 percent of the time. By contrast, subjects playing SQ were still competing at a rate of 90 percent. The inference from these data is clear: Cooperation in a perceptual dilemma is likely to be achieved only if one party initially cooperates unconditionally for a series of encounters.

Voting

Obviously, the vast majority of social dilemma work in political science has involved international conflict. But another issue of interest to political scientists, voting behavior, has been analyzed within a social dilemma framework. Earlier, we argued that government is a public good. You receive all the benefits of government regardless of whether you vote. Voting is typically not a pleasant task; it takes time and energy, and it is highly unlikely our one vote will determine an election. Why do it? Yet many people do vote in every election. Why? Undoubtedly, some people vote out of a sense of duty, but it seems improbable that duty can explain the behavior of more than a few voters. What else might be going on?

An analysis of voting behavior has been done by Palfrey and Rosenthal (1983). Their analysis is based on some key public goods principles, namely, free riding and criticalness. Palfrey and Rosenthal argue that in a democratic country, the immense size of the voting public makes it highly likely that a majority (and minority) favoring a specific political position will exist; the likelihood that all parties will have an equal number of supporters is exceedingly small. Further, individual voters will tend to be aware of whether they are in the majority or minority. As a result, the majority is likely to contain a large number of free riders; if my candidate has a majority of support, there is no reason for me to vote, since he/she will (I assume) win handily. Conversely, the minority voter will believe that, in order for his/her candidate to win, every vote is necessary. In more familiar terms, the minority voter will feel his/her vote is critical. Recall that, when a person feels critical, he/she is very likely to cooperate. Palfrey and Rosenthal conclude that individuals who vote are those who perceive themselves as supporting a minority viewpoint, and consequently feel their votes are critical; individuals who do not vote are those who feel they are in the majority, and want to free ride by letting other majority members vote.

Summary of Games in Political Science

Political scientists have found the prisoner's dilemma and some of its variants to be quite useful in describing and studying international relations. Descriptions of the arms race as a social dilemma have a long history. More recently, the perceptual dilemma has attempted to incorporate beliefs about one's opponent (an especially important component of world politics) into the traditional PDG structure.

Many political scientists who believe the PDG does not adequately describe complex international conflicts have developed alternate game-theoretic models. Security dilemmas and coordination games have been proposed as accurate representations of real world conflicts.

Financial Issues

The general social dilemma paradigm is also quite popular with researchers interested in studying how people conduct economic transactions. We have already discussed the widespread popularity of the public goods paradigm in economics, so it is not all that surprising that other forms of social dilemmas also appeal to these researchers. In fact, the origins of "game theory" (as the formal theory underlying social dilemmas is called) lie in economics, specifically in the 1947 book, *Theory of Games and Economic Behavior* by John von Neumann, a mathematician, and Oskar Morgenstern, an economist. In this section, we will describe research in which economic transactions are modeled as a prisoner's dilemma.

Bargaining and Negotiation

The study of bargaining behavior is very popular with economists, business researchers, and psychologists. How do people with financial interests negotiate with each other so as to reach a satisfactory agreement? Existing research on bargaining is vast, and we will not attempt to provide you with a broad introduction to the area. Instead, we will present some studies of bargaining that use a prisoner's dilemma-type format to test hypotheses.

Table 6.8 shows how a bargaining situation can be represented as a prisoner's dilemma. In this game, the "seller" has a commodity that he/she wishes to dispose of, and the "buyer" wants to acquire that same commodity. Their task is to reach agreement on a selling price for, and possibly quantity of, the commodity. Presumably, the

TABLE 6.8 Bargaining as a Prisoner's Dilemma

	Seller	
Buyer	*Concede*	*Firm*
Concede	Moderate price	High price
Firm	Low price	Stalemate

seller will ask a much higher price than the buyer wants to pay. Thus, in Table 6.8, both the values of the outcomes "high price" and "low price" are opposite for buyer and seller. Both parties can be firm and unyielding with their offer, or concede to the demands of the other party. If one party is firm while the other concedes, the firm party will receive the price (and possibly quantity) he/she originally wanted, and the conceding party will make out very badly. If both are firm, no agreement will be reached (a situation known as a "stalemate") and no merchandise will change hands. Finally, if both concede, a transaction will occur, albeit at a price that neither party originally wanted.

An example of research using this type of bargaining structure was conducted by Komorita and Esser (1975). They were interested in the question of whether the tit-for-tat strategy is effective at producing agreement, compared to "always concede" (similar to all-C) and "never concede" (all-D) strategies. In their study, a subject played the role of buyer, and (unbeknownst to the subject) one of these preprogrammed strategies played the seller. The subject was told that he/she wanted to purchase a used appliance the "seller" wished to dispose of, and that the task was to agree upon a price for the appliance. Both subject and "seller" proposed an initial price for the appliance, and then commenced exchanging offers until an agreement was reached, or 20 exchanges had occurred, at which point a stalemate was declared. (This limit was not known to subjects.) On any given exchange, the subject had two choices: Hold firm or increase the offer by $5 (concession). In the TFT condition, the "seller" matched the subject's action on the next trial; in the "never concede" condition, the "seller" always held firm; and in the "always concede" condition, the "seller" continually decreased the price until it was halved, and then held firm.

Komorita and Esser found TFT to be a very effective means of eliciting agreements. Over 85 percent of all subjects in this condition were able to reach an agreement on a price. By contrast, only about 15 percent of subjects reached an agreement in the "never concede" condition, along with 60 percent in the "always concede" condition. These results are very similar to those later reported by Axelrod (1984), though his All-C strategy never wavered from cooperation.

Bettenhausen and Murnighan (1991) used a prisoner's dilemma to investigate whether a subject's prevailing approach to negotiation (cooperative or competitive) can be altered. This is an important question because, in the real world, bargainers must often decide *how* to negotiate as well as what to negotiate for. In their study, subjects played a number of trials of a prisoner's dilemma that had a high K-value, and thus encouraged cooperation, or a low K-value (encouraged competition). After completion of this game, subjects played a second PDG. In this second game, the task was to negotiate with the other person and reach agreement as to what choices should be made. Bettenhausen and Murnighan manipulated both the type of experience with one's partner (cooperative or competitive game) and the K-value of the new game (high or low).

A number of intriguing results emerged from this study. For example, pairs of cooperative-game subjects often switched to competition if the new game's K-value was low; however, pairs of competitive-game subjects did *not* switch to cooperation if the new K-value was high. Perhaps most interesting were the results of negotiations between partners with different experiences. The competitive-game subject presented a forceful argument for making competitive choices in the new game; the cooperative-game partner argued just as forcefully for cooperative choice. In the majority of cases, the cooperation argument prevailed. Mixed-experience pairs usually made cooperative choices in the second game. Thus, when individuals negotiate over adoption of a competitive or cooperative course of action, cooperation seems to have the edge.

Finally, McCallum and colleagues (McCallum, Harring, Gilmore, Drenan, Chase, Insko, & Thibaut, 1985) used a PDG paradigm to study negotiation behavior between groups. Both individuals and two-person groups were asked to play ten trials of a PDG for money. Before making a choice on any given trial, both individuals/pairs were allowed time to plan a course of action and then to negotiate choices with the opponent. McCallum *et al.* found negotiations between individuals produced more cooperation than between groups. The average individual made the cooperative (C) choice almost 70 percent of the time; by contrast, pairs of subjects cooperated only 38 percent of the time. McCallum *et al.* interpreted this finding as indicating that negotiation teams approach negotiations with a more competitive mindset than an isolated individual.

These studies are by no means exhaustive of all the ways in which the prisoner's dilemma can be used to study bargaining. Such a discussion would fill an entire chapter by itself [in fact, Murnighan (1991) has devoted several chapters to just this topic]. We simply want to illustrate the applicability of the PDG to questions of negotiation behavior.

Other Questions

The work on bargaining is heavily empirical. Much laboratory and field research exists that tests propositions put forth by prisoner's dilemma models of bargaining behavior. For many economic questions, however, it is difficult (if not impossible) to test theory, primarily because it is difficult to accurately simulate a complex financial system in the laboratory. As a result, much of the work done by economists involving social dilemmas is theoretical in nature. Further, this work is often highly mathematical, and is far beyond the scope of this book. Despite this, it is important to be aware of the many issues to which economists have applied social dilemma concepts. Thus, in this section we simply want to give you some examples of these issues.

For many theorists, the prisoner's dilemma (and variants) has been the social dilemma model of choice. Among other areas, the PDG has been used to model rental decisions regarding African-Americans in an all-white neighborhood (Smolensky, Becker, & Molotch, 1968); governmental decisions regarding federal intervention into the marketplace (e.g., "Should a certain industry be regulated?") (Inman, 1987) and provision of financial welfare systems (Buchanan, 1975; Kotlikoff, 1987); the maintenance of partnerships (Radner, Myerson, & Maskin, 1986) and cartels (Green & Porter, 1984); and the effects of long-run versus short-run perspectives on the economy (Fudenberg, Kreps, & Maskin, 1990).

Other paradigms have also proven to be useful for describing economic systems. For example, the public goods paradigm has been used to address patterns of military expenditures by members of the North Atlantic Treaty Organization (NATO) (Sandler & Murdoch, 1990) as well the unification and dissolution of countries (Feinstein, 1992). The resource dilemma has been used to study allocation decisions within a corporation (Mannix & White, 1992), and a new subdiscipline of economics known as "family economics" has arisen to study how family members "harvest" and allocate limited resources provided by the family (e.g., Becker, 1981; Bernheim & Stark, 1988). It would obviously be difficult to test most of these models in a controlled laboratory setting, but they provide the economist with useful explanations of large-scale phenomena.

Summary of Games and Finance

Social dilemmas have proven to be useful for questions of monetary transactions. Much empirical data exist regarding how individuals and groups bargain over economic issues. In addition, prisoner's dilemma and public goods paradigms have been used to model large-scale, real-world financial systems, ranging from NATO to the family.

Biology

It may surprise you to learn that some biologists use social dilemma paradigms as a research tool and gaming as a theoretical construct. In fact, many researchers who study evolution are interested in a question we posed in Chapter 5: "Where does cooperation come from?" We shall examine this often controversial question shortly, but first, let us examine some research addressing whether animals can learn to optimize in a prisoner's dilemma game.

PDG "Played" by Nonhumans

Some experimenters have placed nonhumans into PDG-type situations to determine whether they demonstrate, or can learn, strategic game-playing behaviors. Incredibly, even bacteria have been shown to exhibit what could be called strategic actions in a dilemma-type situation (Ptashne, Johnson, & Pabo, 1982). At a more neurally complex level, Flood, Lendenmann, and Rapoport (1983) had pairs of rats play a prisoner's dilemma game. Each rat was placed in a cage that contained two levers. Pressing a lever caused both levers to be retracted (so that they could not be pressed again) and delivered a pellet of food into the cage. The "payoff" to each rat was the delay between the lever press and food delivery, and was determined by the combination of levers pressed. If a rat did not press a lever within four seconds, no food was delivered to him on that trial. A sample "payoff" matrix is shown in Table 6.9. Flood *et al.* assumed that the desirability of a payoff was inversely related to delay; in other words, the rats most preferred short delays.

TABLE 6.9 Flood *et al.*'s Rat "Payoff" Matrix

| | | Rat 2 | |
		Lever A	Lever B
Rat 1	Lever A	10 sec., 10 sec.	20 sec., 5 sec.
	Lever B	5 sec., 20 sec.	15 sec., 15 sec.

TABLE 6.10 Two Stickleback Fish When Encountering a Predator

| | Stickleback 1 | |
Stickleback 2	Advance	Stay back
Advance	Identify Predator \ Identify Predator	Be killed \ Learn attack distance
Stay Back	Learn Attack Distance \ Be Killed	Do not identify predator \ Do not identify predator

Flood *et al.* put each of twelve rats through about 1000 trials. The average rat registered a choice on 87 percent of the trials. On these trials, the dominating response (press Lever B) was very strong: Ten of the twelve rats chose Lever B at least 75 percent of the time (the average for these rats was 89.7 percent). Of the remaining rats, one chose B 53 percent of the time, the other only 30 percent. In general, then, the rats did not learn that mutual cooperation is jointly more desirable than mutual competition in a PDG situation.

Another example of social dilemma research on animals was conducted by Milinski (1987). He proposed that the PDG can describe some behaviors of stickleback fish. When sticklebacks encounter a possible predator fish, they need to swim relatively close to the possible enemy in order to make a positive identification. Milinski argued that the encounter of this predator by a pair of sticklebacks constitutes a prisoner's dilemma. Table 6.10 describes it in matrix form. After spying the possible enemy, each fish must choose to either advance closer (C) or stay back (D). If both

TABLE 6.11 Swallow Behavior as a Prisoner's Dilemma

Parent	Nonbreeder			
	Passivity		Kill	
Don't Attack	Added Defense of Nest	Learn about nesting site	Low reproductive success	Steal nest
Attack	Scare away threat	Lose status and cannot compete	Waste time	No information about site

sticklebacks cooperate (advance), they can positively identify the predator; if both defect (stay back), they cannot. However, if only one advances, the predator will probably attack and the advancing stickleback will be eaten; by contrast, the stickleback that stayed behind will learn exactly how close it can get to the predator before being attacked. Thus, the D choice (staying back) dominates being cooperative (advance). Milinski provided data to support the hypothesis that one stickleback would advance toward a possible enemy only if a second one did as well. (An advance was considered to be any movement in the direction of the predator.) It should be noted that Milinski did not require the movements to be sequential or simultaneous; the stickleback would simply make frequent checks to see if its partner had also advanced. The fish, then, seem to have been somewhat aware of (and knew to avoid) being suckered.

Finally, Lombardo (1985) studied the behavior of parental and nonbreeding tree swallows. Nonbreeding swallows will often visit the nests of parental swallows to gain information about the nesting site. Lombardo argued that such a situation can be represented as a prisoner's dilemma. Table 6.11 diagrams Lombardo's argument. For a nonbreeder, a cooperative behavior would be to benignly visit the parents' nest; a competitive action would be to lower the parents' chances of successful reproduction (e.g., kill the birdlings). For parents, cooperation would involve letting the nonbreeder investigate the nest; a competitive act would be to attack the nonbreeder. Combinations of these actions could produce the outcomes shown in Table 6.12. For example, mutual cooperation is beneficial to both birds: The nonbreeder gains valuable information about the nesting site, while the parents gain an additional defender of the nest. By contrast, mutual defection is bad: Parents waste valuable parenting time attacking the nonbreeder, while the nonbreeder learns nothing about the nesting site. For both birds, however, defection is the dominant choice. If the parents attack the benign nonbreeder, they will remove a possible threat to their offspring's survival; if the nonbreeder is aggressive toward the cooperative parents, it can steal the entire nest from the parents. Lombardo tested his hypothesis and found the prisoner's dilemma to be an accurate representation of parent-nonbreeder interaction.

Evolution

Game theory and issues of cooperation have also been popular topics with evolutionary biologists. Game theory has been used to model how seemingly incompatible species can come to coexist, and one of the most hotly debated topics in evolutionary science revolves around why people are cooperative. It is worthwhile for us to discuss both areas.

Evolutionary Stability

In many parts of the United States, hawks and doves share the same terrain. Hawks are aggressive, fighting birds; doves are not. When a dove encounters another bird, it will act threatening, but retreat if actual conflict seems likely. The hawk, on the other hand, will physically attack its opponent. It is exceedingly difficult for a dove to defend itself against a hawk attack. Given this, it should be the case that doves will become extinct in areas where they must coexist with hawks. But yet this has not occurred. Why not?

A game-theoretic explanation to this puzzle has been offered. Maynard-Smith and colleagues (e.g., Maynard-Smith, 1974, 1976, 1984; Maynard-Smith & Price, 1973; Parker, 1978, 1984) have argued that, in essence, the hawk-dove problem represents a social dilemma. Table 6.12 presents a matrix description of this dilemma, adapted from Parker (1984). The key to understanding this dilemma lies in the likelihood with which a particular conflict will occur. If there are equal numbers of hawks and doves, then a hawk-dove conflict is moderately likely, and the hawks will do very well. However, with this success comes a negative side effect: The dove population will diminish. As this happens, the likelihood of a hawk-dove conflict decreases, and the likelihood of a hawk-hawk conflict increases. These conflicts produce injury and death and serve to

TABLE 6.12 The Hawk-Dove Dilemma

Bird 2	Bird 1	
	Hawk	*Dove*
Hawk	Injury / Injury	Lose / Win
Dove	Win / Lose	Threaten / Threaten

decrease the hawk population. Doves, however, will propagate. If the dove population gets too large relative to hawks (a likely prospect, since dove-dove conflicts do not thin the dove population), the hawk population will grow because hawks will be able to avoid conflicts with their own species. Thus, whether or not a species becomes extinct from predation is a function of the probability of encountering the predator. But this analysis would suggest that we should see sharp fluctuations in the populations of various species, yet we do not. Why not?

To explain this lack of fluctuation, Maynard-Smith introduced the concept of an *evolutionarily stable strategy* (ESS). An ESS is a choice strategy such that, if all members of the group employ it, a rare alternative (or "mutant") strategy cannot "invade" the group. A strategy is considered to have invaded a group when it succeeds (receives a higher payoff) in competition with the other strategy. To illustrate, let's assume the initial existence of an all-dove population. In other words, doves will always have a conflict with other doves. (This strategy is termed a "pure" one because it involves making a single choice 100 percent of the time.) What happens if a single hawk joins the group? The hawk will be very successful (because it can only fight doves) and other hawks will soon join the group. In other words, the all-dove strategy has been invaded by hawks. Thus, all-dove is not an ESS. Clearly, the birds (and other species) have identified a combination of hawks and doves (called a "mixed" strategy) such that the frequencies of hawk-hawk, hawk-dove, and dove-dove conflicts hold both populations stable. There is some empirical evidence for ESSs among insects (e.g., Brockmann, Grafen, & Dawkins, 1979; Parker, 1970). How ESSs evolve is beyond the scope of this book, but it is a question of interest to evolutionary theorists.

The Evolution of Cooperation

You now know that cooperation is a concept central to the study of social dilemmas. One of the most heavily debated issues in biology centers around *where* cooperation comes from. In economics, a "rational" person is one who always looks out for his/her own best interests. This ethic was probably even more true in prehistoric times, when a failure to act in a self-interested manner could easily mean death. Similarly, many psychological theories posit that the driving force behind much of human behavior involves self-interest: The satisfaction of needs, the desire to experience pleasure, or the desire for things of positive valence (Campbell, 1975). Given this, how could cooperation have ever developed? There are two schools of thought regarding this issue. One argues that cooperation evolved because it is "functional." The other questions the accuracy of our definition of rationality, arguing that humans are basically "social" and cooperate as a matter of course.

The Practicality of Cooperation

Many evolutionary theorists believe that selfish humans developed cooperation as a mechanism to further their own interests. These theories are often called "egoistic incentive (EI)" theories. Some (e.g., Alexander, 1987; Dawkins, 1976) go so far as to argue that cooperation exists to propagate one's genes and to ensure that one's genetic traits will not die out. In order to accomplish this, one must make sure that those with similar genetic makeups (e.g., relatives) survive. Thus, these theories predict that cooperation will only occur if the parties are sufficiently genetically related.

Less severely, Trivers (1971) suggested that individuals cooperate because, at some future time, the target of our cooperation may return the favor. However, if the person we help does not plan on reciprocating (Trivers called this kind of person a *nonaltruist*), their exploitation of us will make us less likely to be cooperative in the future. Trivers based his argument on prisoner's dilemma principles: If you receive the Sucker's payoff on trial n, you will probably switch to defection on trial $n + 1$.

Trivers' argument also has a genetic base. According to Trivers, the initial decision regarding whether or not to cooperate is the result of a genetic cost-benefit analysis: The costs of cooperation involve the extent to which our ability to reproduce our genes is adversely affected; the benefits are the extent to which the target's ability to reproduce his/her genes is increased. Note that Trivers' emphasis is still on selfish interests. If we initiate cooperation, it is because we expect to receive help in the future. If we are the target of a cooperative behavior, it is in our best interests to reciprocate that behavior so as to ensure that the person will help us again.

An extension of Trivers' theory was proposed by Hoffman (1981). He argued that the mechanism underlying cooperation is not reciprocity, but rather empathy. (*Empathy* is defined as the vicarious emotional response of one person to another's emotional experience.) Hoffman presented evidence to support his hypothesis. For example, infants as young as 1–day respond empathically to another person in distress; empathic responses seem to have a neural, involuntary basis; and empathic arousal precedes helping behavior and diminishes after the act. Similarly, Simon (1990) argues that cooperation has its basis in *docility,* or tolerance of exploitation. Simon suggests that docility is a positive trait because society can "put a tax" on it; that is, society can exploit docile individuals and get them to produce socially beneficial behaviors. Because docility is a positive trait, it will be selected for in the evolutionary process, and soon all members of society will possess the trait. Thus, eventually everyone will behave in a manner that helps others, and mutual cooperation will be achieved.

Axelrod (1984; Axelrod & Hamilton, 1981) proposed an explanation that incorporates elements of both the purely genetic and Trivers' theories. He argued that initially, organisms (human and nonhuman) cooperate only with those to whom they are closely genetically related. As the group grows, individuals will be less able to determine to whom they are genetically related and will (due to uncertainty about the other's genetic history) begin to cooperate with nonrelated organisms. The other organism, being also uncertain of the individual's genetics, will also cooperate. This interaction does not extend the genetic trait life of either organism, but it does produce positive payoffs for both. Thus, cooperation becomes generalized.

For any two interacting organisms, there is a probability w that they will encounter each other again in the future. If w is small (i.e., it is very unlikely that the organisms will ever interact again, and this is similar to a prisoner's dilemma played only once), then unconditional noncooperation is an ESS and individuals with cooperative tendencies will be selected out of the population. However, if w is large (making future interaction likely), and organisms do not know how many more times they will interact, then organisms can reflect upon the pattern of past interactions to develop strategic behaviors. As we know from the results of Axelrod's computer tournament (see Chapter 2), strategic cooperators can achieve reasonably high payoffs (and thus survive) from repeated interactions. Axelrod argued that, in most groups of organisms, w is relatively high; as a result, cooperators exist in all species. Axelrod's theory is obviously based on egoistic incentives: Initially, organisms are trying to prolong the life of their own genetic traits; later, they are cooperating to realize some positive personal payoff.

Sociality as Rationality

All of these explanations of the origin of cooperation assume that organisms are basically hedonistic; in other words, they want to maximize personal benefit whenever possible. A second, relatively recent school of thought argues that humans are *not* by nature selfish beings. The economist Sen (1977) first claimed that there are many instances of human behavior that cannot easily be explained by assuming that people are trying to maximize personal benefit. The most extreme example is the soldier who throws himself on a grenade to save his comrades. It can be argued that the person is trying to achieve glory, but glory would not seem to be of much use to a dead man. A more common example would be the citizen who votes to raise taxes. Many other theorists have since expanded Sen's basic argument (see Mansbridge, 1989).

Some investigators have explained such patterns of behavior by suggesting that the human brain, which evolved to address one class of problems (e.g., food-gathering), is ill-equipped to deal with the more complex problems of today (e.g., Campbell, 1986). A stronger proposition has been offered by Caporael, Dawes, Orbell, and van de Kragt (1989; see also Dawes, 1991). They suggest that man is not basically selfish, but basically social. The crux of their "sociality" argument is that, in prehistoric times, a lone individual simply could not survive. Imagine a single caveman trying to kill a woolly mammoth, or carrying fresh meat across a field with predators nearby. Because of this, humans were forced to live in groups. Such groups were limited in size, though; a woolly mammoth can only feed so many people. Thus, humans not only had to live in groups, but also had to get along with other group members, or risk being expelled from the group. Cooperation thus became the means by which group membership was maintained, and as a result became part of our social being.

Caporael *et al.* support their thesis by citing the series of studies done by Dawes, Orbell, and van de Kragt that we discussed in Chapter 3. You will recall that Dawes, Orbell, and van de Kragt found discussion to be an effective mechanism for increasing contribution to a public good. In one study (van de Kragt *et al.*, 1986), each member of a five-person group received the public good if *the other four members* contributed toward its provision. The individual's action had absolutely no effect on whether he/she received the good. In this situation, contributing cannot benefit the individual in any way, and according to the egoistic incentive line of reasoning, there should be no contribution. Yet 96 percent of van de Kragt *et al.*'s subjects did in fact contribute when they were allowed to discuss the game. It would seem difficult to explain this finding from an EI (egoistic incentives) point of view.

Frank (1989) has extended Caporael *et al.*'s hypothesis by arguing that cooperation can be made an ESS. Frank suggests that cooperators and defectors can easily be distinguished from one another by careful scrutiny. This is because cooperators exhibit features that are difficult to fake. For example, Frank argues that cooperators have a sincere manner and cannot conceal a lie. If we are willing to take the time and scrutinize the manner of all other group members, it will become obvious with whom we should and should not interact.

Summary of Games in Biology

Prisoner's dilemmas have been found to be accurate models of some aspects of animal behavior. In more artificial situations, however, some animals seem unable to learn the benefits of cooperation, and continue to make defecting choices even after 1000 trials.

Game theoretic principles have figured strongly into some aspects of evolution theory. For example, game theory has been used to explain how hostile species can continue to coexist. A hotly debated topic among evolution theorists involves how humans came to be cooperative. The traditional line of reasoning argues that humans cooperate for selfish reasons. A more recent counterargument posits that man has by necessity always had to be a social being, a lifestyle that requires being cooperative.

Summary and Conclusions

Examples of Social Dilemmas
   Fishing in the Atlantic Ocean
   Steam Power
   Incentive Programs
   Energy Conservation

Future Research on Social Dilemmas
   Applied Research
   Rectifying Discrepant Findings
   Interdisciplinary Work

Throughout this book, we have emphasized the practical as well as the theoretical importance of social dilemma research. From a purely scientific standpoint, this work has provided us with revealing insights into the nature of human interaction and interdependence. But we have also argued that this research is directly relevant to the real world. Particularly in the areas of public goods and social traps, we have stressed the multitude of real examples of social dilemmas, and pointed out whether proposed ''solutions'' to these dilemmas are realistic, in the sense that they could easily be adopted by real-world managers of these goods. We shall end our presentation of social dilemma work by demonstrating what we are talking about: we want to describe some actual examples of social dilemmas in society, and show how they might be solved using basic research findings. After discussing a number of examples, we will conclude this discussion by suggesting some future directions for social dilemmas research.

Examples of Social Dilemmas

We shall start by summarizing some actual social dilemmas that have been reported by scientists. This is by no means a complete list of all the real dilemmas that have been reported, and we simply offer a few examples to illustrate the pervasiveness of real-world social dilemmas.

Fishing in the Atlantic Ocean

Allen and McGlade (1987) used the social trap paradigm to describe the plight of Canadian fishers, and to demonstrate how the fishers used a basic resource dilemma concept to resolve their problem. Fish are a replenishable resource. Fishers will catch many of them, but the remaining fish will breed and produce offspring every year. Of course, the fishers have a financial incentive to catch fish, since they can sell their catches for food and oil. However, if a fishers' catch is too large, he/she will suffer a financial setback because the unsold fish will quickly rot. Thus, there is a financial harvest limit on the fish. However, Allen and McGlade observed that, at the start of the 1980's, demand for fish grew dramatically. The direct result of this increase in demand was to raise the harvest limit: now, more fish can be sold. Soon, all fishers began to harvest fish at or near this new, higher limit. You will recall from Chapter 4 what happens when all group members act this way—the resource depletes very quickly. This is exactly what happened. Soon, the stock of fish was dangerously low.

How was the dilemma solved? The fishers recognized that their catch rates had to be balanced with the birth rate of the fish. In other words, the fishers realized that an optimal harvest level existed. Catch rates were scaled back accordingly, and the pool of fish stabilized (though it was of course smaller than before).

Steam Power

In northern California there are a number of fumaroles, or holes in the ground from which steam and hot water issue. Fumaroles are created when underground water hits magma, or molten rock. Magma makes the water boil, which of course produces steam. As with any water table, fumarole water is partially replenished by rainfall and mountain runoff. We all know that steam pressure can act as a power source, and geophysicists have suggested that the steam from fumaroles be tapped as an inexpensive source of power.

Richard Kerr (1991) has observed that this steam presents a social trap. Cheap sources of power are in very high demand, and as such the temptation is great for everyone to tap into the source. However, in order to maintain a constant level of pressure, water must be replenished at a steady rate. The pressure was heavily used: as soon as the state government allowed commercial use of fumaroles, almost 40 companies began tapping the steam. But, California's severe drought meant that the fumarole water was being replenished at an exceedingly low rate. The end result was that steam was drawn heavily and replenishment was so minor that steam pressure fell to half its original level, and the generators powered by the steam ceased working. The power companies that did not go out of business have had to undertake expensive measures to make the generators run again, and the cheap source of power is no longer cheap.

How could we solve this dilemma? First, we would need to temporarily halt use of the steam until the fumarole water had been replenished to a sufficient level. (In fact, the California government has attempted to hasten the replenishment rate by filling the fumaroles with unconsumable waste water.) After the water is replenished, we could adopt a structural solution and impose a leader system. Instead of allowing each company to decide how much steam pressure they will use, the state government could dictate and regulate the maximum amount of steam any given company can use. Recall from Chapter 4 that group members who have experienced overuse will generally be accepting of a leader system, so such a solution would probably not encounter much resistance from the companies.

Incentive Programs

Many companies (in America, at least) have in place incentive programs to motivate workers. The aim of these programs is to spur productivity by offering some kind of reward to those who produce at a certain level. Many students of organizations (e.g., Laver, 1981; Spicer, 1985; see also Roth, 1991) have demonstrated that these programs actually place workers into a social dilemma situation. Consider a group-based incentive program. This type of program establishes a criterion for a work group to meet. If the total output of all workers in the group is above a certain amount, all group members will receive the rewards (a bonus). It should be immediately apparent to you that such a program is exactly like a minimal contributing set of a public good. If a number of group members work hard enough to produce the required amount (i.e., cooperate), then all will get the bonus, even those who did not work hard. Just as in a typical public good, we would expect this type of incentive program to cause free riding.

Rutte (1990) reported an actual instance of such a dilemma. She described a Dutch bank where teams of keypunch operators were given the incentive of going home as soon as all of the day's work was completed. At the start of the day, work would be divided equally among all teams. After lunch, the remaining work would be divided equally. If everyone works hard (cooperates), all the work will be done quickly, and all can go home very early. However, if a team does not work hard (defects), their remaining work will be split among the others after lunch. Thus, one can free ride; if every team works hard except mine, they will all have to help with our work after lunch. Of course, if everyone acts in this way, no one will be able to go home early, so complete defection is worse than complete cooperation.

Rutte observed that most of the teams were free riders, the incentive was rarely achieved, and the workplace atmosphere was quite unpleasant. The company solved the problem by changing the reward structure. As soon as a team finished its work, the members could leave, regardless of how far other teams had progressed. This is very similar to a "fair share" requirement (minimize "greed"). Since the work is divided equally, this means that all teams start with an equal "endowment" of work. If a team contributes its endowment (i.e., completes its work), it gets the good (going home early). However, a team cannot go home until it contributes. Thus, a team must do its fair share of work in order to realize the good.

Energy Conservation

Energy use has long been thought of as a social dilemma (e.g., Shippee, 1980; Stern & Gardner, 1981). Energy is a resource, and as with any social trap, the short-term incentive is to consume a great amount of it. However, in the long run such heavy consumption will almost inevitably lead to shortages and higher prices. Samuelson (1991) looked at the problem and proposed some techniques for making energy consumption more optimal. He argued that conservation could most effectively be encouraged by enhancing group identity. In fact, Samuelson reviewed a number of examples of successful conservation programs, and observed that all involved some element of group identity. You will recall from our discussion of social traps that enhanced group identity should lead members to perform behaviors that benefit the group rather than just themselves. His recommendation involves organizing neighborhoods into small groups, offering financial incentives to successfully conserving groups, or holding contests between groups. One's immediate reaction to this plan is that it would encourage free riding; note that it is very similar to the group incentive programs we just discussed. To counter this, Samuelson suggested that each group member's electricity meter be monitored on a daily basis, and the daily use rates made public through a newsletter. This would immediately identify free riders and make others aware of who is free riding.

Future Research on Social Dilemmas

We conclude our text by pointing out some research areas that require more work. It should be clear by now that there is still much to be learned about behavior in social dilemmas, and we will not attempt to summarize all of these areas. We shall instead focus on topics about which information is particularly lacking.

Applied Research

The area about which we know almost nothing is the extent to which laboratory solutions to social dilemmas can be generalized to real world problems (Kerr, 1990). We are aware of no studies that have attempted to implement empirical solutions in an actual dilemma situation. Few researchers have even examined real dilemmas and devised specific solutions in the manner of Samuelson (1991). Given that many social dilemma researchers state that they are attracted to the problem because of its social relevance, we need to evaluate how successful we have been in addressing these real problems. Social psychology is often criticized for studying abstract questions, and this would seem to be an ideal opportunity to put much of that criticism to rest.

Rectifying Discrepant Findings

Throughout this book we reported cases in which competing hypotheses were proposed to explain cooperative behavior. For example, in Chapter 2 we noted that deindividuation theorists assume that cooperation can be facilitated by minimizing the salience of group membership, while group identity theorists argue that cooperation is improved by *enhancing* the salience of the group. There are many other such situations in dilemma research. We need to clarify these discrepant predictions by conducting some crucial tests of the hypotheses. Doing so will more sharply define the variables that affect cooperative behavior.

Interdisciplinary Work

Finally, there needs to be more collaboration between the various disciplines interested in social dilemmas. We pointed out in Chapter 6 just how widespread this interest is. Unfortunately, there seems to be little communication between disciplines, and as a result, researchers spend too much time discovering what someone in another discipline already knew. This is not to say that there is complete ignorance of other disciplines, but rather to encourage researchers in all areas to read social dilemma work by those other than their colleagues.

REFERENCES

Alcock, J. E., & Mansell, D. (1977) Predisposition and behavior in a collective dilemma. *Journal of Conflict Resolution, 21,* 443–457.

Alexander, R. D. (1987) *The biology of moral systems.* Hawthorne, NY: Aldine de Gruyter.

Allen, P. M., & McGlade, J. M. (1987) Modelling complex human systems: A fisheries example. *European Journal of Operations Research, 30,* 147–167.

Allison, S. T., McQueen, L. R., & Schaerfl, L. M. (1992) Social decision making processes and the equal partitionment of shared resources. *Journal of Experimental Social Psychology, 28,* 23–42.

Allison, S. T., & Messick, D. M. (1985) Effects of experience on performance in a replenishable resource trap. *Journal of Personality and Social Psychology, 49,* 943–948.

Allison, S. T., & Messick, D. M. (1990) Social decision heuristics in the use of shared resources. *Journal of Behavioral Decision Making, 3,* 195–204.

Anderton, C. H. (1989) Arms race modeling: Problems and prospects. *Journal of Conflict Resolution, 33,* 346–367.

Andreoni, J. (1988) Why free ride? Strategies and learning in public goods experiments. *Journal of Public Economics, 37,* 291–304.

Arabie, P., Carroll, J. D., & DeSarbo, W. S. (1987) *Three-way scaling and clustering.* Sage University Paper series on Quantitative Applications in the Social Sciences, no. 65. Beverly Hills, CA: Sage.

Arkes, H. R., & Blumer, C. (1985) The psychology of sunk cost. *Organizational Behavior and Human Decision Processes, 35,* 124–140.

Axelrod, R. (1984) *The evolution of cooperation.* New York: Basic Books.

Axelrod, R., & Dion, D. (1988) The further evolution of cooperation. *Science, 242,* 1385–1390.

Axelrod, R., & Hamilton, W. D. (1981) The evolution of cooperation. *Science, 211,* 1390–1396.

Bandura, A. (1986) *Social foundations of thought and action.* Englewood Cliffs, NJ: Prentice-Hall.

Barry, B., & Hardin, R. (1982) *Rational man and irrational society?* Beverly Hills, CA: Sage.

Baxter, G. W. Jr. (1972) Personality and attitudinal characteristics in cooperation in two-person games: A review. In L. S. Wrightsman, J. O'Connor, & N. J. Baker (eds), *Cooperation and competition* (pp. 97–103). Belmont, CA: Brooks-Cole.

Becker, G. S. (1981) *A treatise on the family.* Cambridge: Harvard U. Press.

Beggan, J. K., Messick, D. M., & Allison, S. T. (1988) Social values and egocentric bias: Two tests of the might over morality hypothesis. *Journal of Personality & Social Psychology, 55,* 606–611.

Bell, P. A., Petersen, T. R., & Hautaluoma, J. E. (1989) The effect of punishment probability on overconsumption and stealing in a simulated commons. *Journal of Applied Social Psychology, 19,* 1483–1495.

Bernheim, B. D., & Stark, O. (1988) Altruism within the family reconsidered: Do nice guys finish last? *American Economic Review, 78,* 1034–1045.

Bettenhausen, K. L., & Murnighan, J. K. (1991) Developing and challenging a group norm: Interpersonal cooperation and structural competition. *Administrative Science Quarterly, 36,* 20–35.

Bixenstine, V. E., Levitt, C. A., & Wilson, K. V. (1966) Collaboration among six persons in a prisoner's dilemma game. *Journal of Conflict Resolution, 10,* 488–496.

Blau, P. M. (1964) *Exchange and power in social life.* New York: Wiley.

Bonacich, P. (1972) Norms and cohesion as adaptive responses to potential conflict: An experimental study. *Sociometry, 35,* 357–375.

Bonacich, P. (1976) Secrecy and solidarity. *Sociometry, 39,* 200–208.

Bornstein, G. (1992) The free-rider problem in intergroup conflicts over step-level and continuous public goods. *Journal of Personality & Social Psychology, 62,* 597–606.

Bornstein, G., Crum, L., Wittenbraker, J., Harring, K., Insko, C. A., & Thibaut, J. (1983) On the measurement of social orientations in the minimal group paradigm. *European Journal Of Social Psychology, 13,* 321–350.

Bornstein, G., & Rapoport, Am. (1988) Intergroup competition for the provision of step-level public goods: Effects of preplay communication. *European Journal of Social Psychology, 18,* 125–144.

Bornstein, G., Rapoport, Am., Kerpel, L., & Katz, T. (1989) Within- and between-group communication in intergroup competition for public goods. *Journal of Experimental Social Psychology, 25,* 422–431.

Brams, S. J. (1975) Newcomb's problem and the prisoner's dilemma. *Journal of Conflict Resolution, 19,* 596–612.

Brams, S. J. (1976) *Paradoxes in politics.* New York: The Free Press.

Brams, S. J. (1985) *Superpower games.* New Haven, CT: Yale U. Press.

Brams, S. J., David, M. D., & Straffin, P. D. (1979) The geometry of the arms race. *International Studies Quarterly, 23,* 567–588.

Brams, S. J., & Kilgour, D. M. (1988) *Game theory and national security.* New York: Basil Blackwell.

Braver, S. R., & Wilson, L. A. (1986) Choices in social dilemmas: Effects of communication within subgroups. *Journal of Conflict Resolution, 30,* 51–62.

Brechner, K. C. (1977) An experimental analysis of social traps. *Journal of Experimental Social Psychology, 13,* 552–564.

Brewer, M. B. (1979) In-group bias in the minimal intergroup situation: A cognitive-motivational analysis. *Psychological Bulletin, 86,* 307–324.

Brewer, M. B. (1981) Ethnocentrism and its role in interpersonal trust. In M. B. Brewer & B. E. Collins (eds), *Scientific inquiry in the social sciences* (pp. 345–360). New York: Jossey-Bass.

Brewer, M. B., & Kramer, R. M. (1986) Choice behavior in social dilemmas: Effects of social identity, group size, and decision framing. *Journal of Personality and Social Psychology, 50,* 543–549.

Brockmann, H. J., Grafen, A., & Dawkins, R. (1979) Evolutionarily stable nesting strategy in a digger wasp. *Journal of Theoretical Biology, 77,* 473–496.

Brockner, J., Rubin, J. Z., & Lang, E. (1981) Face-saving and entrapment. *Journal of Experimental Social Psychology, 17,* 68–79.

Brubaker, E. R. (1975) Free ride, free revelation, or golden rule? *Journal of Law and Economics, 18,* 147–161.

Buchanan, J. M. (1975) The Samaritan's dilemma. In E. S. Phelps (ed), *Altruism, morality, and economic theory* (pp. 71–85). New York: Russell Sage Foundation.

Buchanan, J. M., & Tullock, H. (1962) *The calculus of consent.* Ann Arbor: U. of Michigan Press.

Campbell, D. T. (1975) On the conflicts between biological and social evolution and between psychology and moral tradition. *American Psychologist, 30,* 1103–1126.

Campbell, D. T. (1986) Rationality and utility from the standpoint of evolutionary biology. *Journal of Business, 59,* 355–364.

Caporael, L. R., Dawes, R. M., Orbell, J. M., & van de Kragt, A. J. C. (1989) Selfishness examined: Cooperation in the absence of egoistic incentives. *Behavioral and Brain Sciences, 12,* 683–699.

Conlon, E. J., & Wolf, G. (1980) The moderating effects of strategy, visibility, and involvement on allocation behavior: An extension of Staw's escalation paradigm. *Organizational Behavior and Human Performance, 26,* 172–192.

Cross, J. G., & Guyer, M. J. (1980) *Social traps.* Ann Arbor: U. of Michigan Press.

Darley, J. M., & Latane, B. (1968) Bystander intervention in emergencies: Diffusion of responsibility. *Journal of Personality and Social Psychology, 8,* 377–383.

Dawes, R. M. (1975) Formal models of dilemmas in social decision-making. In M. F. Kaplan & S. Schwartz (eds), *Human judgment and decision processes* (pp. 87–108). New York: Academic Press.

Dawes, R. M. (1980) Social dilemmas. *Annual Review of Psychology, 31,* 169–193.

Dawes, R. M. (1988) *Rational choice in an uncertain world.* San Diego: Harcourt Brace Jovanovich.

Dawes, R. M. (1990) Social dilemmas, economic self-interest, and evolutionary theory. In D. R. Brown & J .E. K. Smith (eds), *Frontiers of mathematical psychology* (pp. 53–79). New York: Springer-Verlag.

Dawes, R. M., McTavish, J., & Shaklee, H. (1977) Behavior, communication, and assumptions about other people's behavior in a commons dilemma situation. *Journal of Personality and Social Psychology, 35,* 1–11.

Dawes, R. M., Orbell, J. M., Simmons, R. T., & van de Kragt, A. J. C. (1986) Organizing groups for collective action. *American Political Science Review, 80,* 1171–1185.

Dawes, R. M., van de Kragt, A. J. C., & Orbell, J. M. (1988) Not me or thee but we: The importance of group identity in eliciting cooperation in dilemma situations. *Acta Psychologica, 68,* 83–97.

Dawkins, R. (1976) *The selfish gene.* Oxford: Oxford U. Press.

Deutsch, M. (1949) A theory of cooperation and competition. *Human Relations, 2,* 129–152.

Deutsch, M. (1958) Trust and suspicion. *Journal of Conflict Resolution, 2,* 265–279.

Deutsch, M. (1960a) The effect of motivational orientation upon trust and suspicion. *Human Relations, 13,* 123–139.

Deutsch, M. (1960b) Trust, trustworthiness, and the F-Scale. *Journal of Abnormal and Social Psychology, 61,* 138–140.

Deutsch, M. (1975) Equity, equality, and need: What determines which value will be used as the basis of distributive justice? *Journal of Social Issues, 31,* 137–149.

Diekmann, A. (1985) Volunteer's dilemma. *Journal of Conflict Resolution, 29,* 605–610.

Diekmann, A. (1986) Volunteer's dilemma: A social trap without a dominant strategy and some empirical results. In A. Diekmann & P. Mitter (eds), *Paradoxical effects of social behavior* (pp. 187–197). Heidelberg: Physica Verlag.

Downs, G. W., & Rocke, D. M. (1987) Tacit bargaining and arms control. *World Politics, 39,* 297–325.

Downs, G. W., Rocke, D. M., & Siverson, R. M. (1985) Arms races and cooperation. *World Politics, 38,* 118–146.

Edney, J. J. (1980) The commons problem: Alternative perspectives. *American Psychologist, 35,* 131–150.

Edney, J. J., & Harper, C. S. (1978) Heroism in a resource crisis: A simulation study. *Environmental Management, 2,* 523–527.

Erev, I., & Rapoport, Am. (1990) Provision of step-level public goods: The sequential contribution mechanism. *Journal of Conflict Resolution, 34,* 401–425.

Feinstein, J. S. (1992) Public-good provision and political stability in Europe. *American Economic Review Papers and Proceedings, 82,* 323–329.

Festinger, L., Pepitone, A., & Newcomb, T. (1952) Some consequences of deindividuation in a group. *Journal of Abnormal & Social Psychology, 47,* 383–389.

Fitzgerald, M. A., & Frankie, G. H. (1982) The effects of age and communication on cooperation and competition in childhood and adolescence. *Journal of Genetic Psychology, 141,* 295–296.

Flood, M., Lendenmann, K., & Rapoport, An. (1983) 2 x 2 games played by rats: Different delays of reinforcement payoffs. *Behavioral Science, 28,* 65–78.

Fox, J., & Guyer, M. (1977) Group size and others' strategy in an n-person game. *Journal of Conflict Resolution, 21,* 323–338.

Fox, J., & Guyer, M. (1978) "Public" choice and cooperation in n-person prisoner's dilemma. *Journal of Conflict Resolution, 22,* 469–481.

Frank, R. H. (1989) Honesty as an evolutionary stable strategy. *Behavioral and Brain Sciences, 12,* 705–706.

Frei, D. (1986) *Perceived images.* Totowa, NJ: Rowman & Allanheld.

Fudenberg, D., Kreps, D. M., & Maskin, E. S. (1990) Repeated games with long-run and short-run players. *Review of Economic Studies, 57,* 555–573.

Garland, H., Sandefur, C. A., & Rogers, A. C. (1990) De-escalation of commitment in oil exploration: When sunk costs and negative feedback coincide. *Journal of Applied Psychology, 75,* 721–727.

Gilbert, M. (1984) Coordination problems and the evolution of behavior. *Behavioral and Brain Sciences, 7,* 106–107.

Gordon, R., & Pelkmans, J. (1979) *Challenges to interdependent economies.* New York: McGraw-Hill.

Green, E., & Porter, R. (1984) Noncooperative collusion under imperfect price information. *Econometrica, 52,* 87–100.

Griesinger, D. W., & Livingston, J. W. Jr. (1973) Toward a model of interpersonal motivation in experimental games. *Behavioral Science, 18,* 173–188.

Guyer, M., Fox, J., & Hamburger, H. (1973) Format effects in the prisoner's dilemma. *Journal of Conflict Resolution, 17,* 719–744.

Halpern, J. Y. (1986) Reasoning about knowledge: An overview. In J. Y. Halpern (ed), *Reasoning about knowledge* (pp. 1–18). New York: Morgan Kaufmann.

Hamburger, H. (1973) N-person prisoner's dilemma. *Journal of Mathematical Psychology, 3,* 27–48.

Hamburger, H., Guyer, M., & Fox, J. (1975) Group size and cooperation. *Journal of Conflict Resolution, 19,* 503–531.

Hardin, G. (1968) The tragedy of the commons. *Science, 162,* 1243–1248.

Hardin, G. (1977) Rewards of pejoristic thinking. In G. Hardin & J. Baden (eds), *Managing the commons* (pp. 126–134). San Francisco: Freeman.

Hardin, R. (1983) Unilateral versus mutual disarmament. *Philosophy and Public Affairs, 12,* 236–254.

Harford, T., & Solomon, L. (1967) "Reformed sinner" and "lapsed saint" strategies in the prisoner's dilemma game. *Journal of Conflict Resolution, 11,* 104–109.

Harkins, S. G., & Szymanski, K. (1989) Social loafing and group evaluation. *Journal of Personality and Social Psychology, 56,* 934–941.

Harris, R. J., & Joyce, M. A. (1980) What's fair? It depends on how you phrase the question. *Journal of Personality and Social Psychology, 38,* 165–170.

Harrison, G. W., & Hirshleifer, J. (1989) An experimental evaluation of weakest-link/best-shot models of public goods. *Journal of Political Economics, 97,* 201–225.

Head, J. G. (1962) Public goods and public policy. *Public Finance, 17,* 197–221.

Hepworth, J. T., & West, S. G. (1988) Lynchings and the economy: A time-series reanalysis of Hovland and Sears (1940). *Journal of Personality & Social Psychology, 55,* 239–247.

Hobbes, T. (1651/1939) *Leviathan.* New York: Modern Library.

Hoffman, M.L. (1981) Is altruism part of human nature? *Journal of Personality and Social Psychology, 40,* 121–137.

Hogan, R., & Nicholson, R. A. (1988) The meaning of personality test scores. *American Psychologist, 43,* 621–626.

Homans, G. C. (1961) *Social behavior: Its elementary forms.* New York: Harcourt, Brace, & World.

Inman, R. P. (1987) Markets, governments, and the "new" political economy. In A. J. Auerbach & M. Feldstein (eds), *Handbook of public economics* (pp. 647–777). Amsterdam: North Holland.

Isaac, R. M., McCue, K. F., & Plott, C. R. (1985) Public goods provision in an experimental environment. *Journal of Public Economics, 26,* 51–74.

Isaac, R. M., & Walker, J. M. (1988a) Communication and free-riding behavior: The voluntary contribution mechanism. *Economic Inquiry, 6,* 585–608.

Isaac, R. M., & Walker, J. M. (1988b) Group size effects in public goods provision: The voluntary contributions mechanism. *Quarterly Journal of Economics, 103,* 179–199.

Isard, W., & Anderton, C. H. (1985) Arms race models: A survey and synthesis. *Conflict Management and Peace Science, 8,* 27–98.

Jerdee, T., & Rosen, B. (1974) Effects of opportunity to communicate and visibility of individual decisions on behavior in the common interest. *Journal of Applied Psychology, 5,* 712–716.

Jervis, R. (1978) Cooperation under the security dilemma. *World Politics, 30,* 167–214.

Jorgenson, D. O., & Papciak, A. S. (1981) The effects of communication, resource feedback, and identifiability on behavior in a simulated commons. *Journal of Experimental Social Psychology, 17,* 373–385.

Kagan, S., & Madsen, M. C. (1971) Cooperation and competition of Mexican, Mexican-American, and Anglo-American children of two ages under four instructional sets. *Developmental Psychology, 5,* 32–39.

Kagan, S., & Madsen, M. C. (1972) Rivalry in Anglo-American and Mexican children of two ages. *Journal of Personality and Social Psychology, 24,* 214–220.

Kahn, A., Hottes, J., & Davis, W. L. (1971) Cooperation and optimal responding in the prisoner's dilemma game: Effects of sex and physical attractiveness. *Journal of Personality and Social Psychology, 17,* 267–279.

Kahneman, D., Slovic, P., & Tversky, A. (1982) *Judgement under uncertainty.* Cambridge: Cambridge U. Press.

Kahneman, D., & Tversky, A. (1979) Prospect theory: An analysis of decision under risk. *Econometrica, 47,* 263–291.

Kelley, H. H., & Grzelak, J. (1972) Conflict between individual and common interest in an n-person relationship. *Journal of Personality and Social Psychology, 21,* 190–197.

Kelley, H. H., & Stahelski, A. J. (1970a) Social interaction basis of cooperators' and competitors' beliefs about others. *Journal of Personality and Social Psychology, 16,* 66–91.

Kelley, H. H., & Stahelski, A. J. (1970b) The inference of intentions from moves in the prisoner's dilemma game. *Journal of Experimental Social Psychology, 6,* 401–419.

Kelley, H. H., & Thibaut, J. W. (1978) *Interpersonal relations*. New York: Wiley.

Kelley, H. H., Thibaut, J. W., Radloff, R., & Mundy, D. (1962) The development of cooperation in the "minimal social situation." *Psychological Monographs, 76,* whole no. 538.

Kerr, N. L. (1983) Motivation losses in small groups: A social dilemma analysis. *Journal of Personality and Social Psychology, 45,* 819–828.

Kerr, N. L. (1989) Illusions of efficacy: The effects of group size on perceived efficacy in social dilemmas. *Journal of Experimental Social Psychology, 25,* 287–313.

Kerr, N. L. (1990) Applied perspectives on social and temporal dilemmas: An introduction. *Social Behavior, 5,* 201–205.

Kerr, N. L. (1992) Efficacy as a causal and moderating variable in social dilemmas. In W. B. G. Liebrand, D. M. Messick, & H. A. M. Wilke (eds), *Social dilemmas* (pp. 59–80). New York: Pergamon Press.

Kerr, N. L., & Bruun, S. E. (1981) Ringelmann revisited: Alternative explanations for the social loafing effect. *Personality and Social Psychology Bulletin, 7,* 224–231.

Kerr, N. L., & Bruun, S. E. (1983) Dispensability of member effort and group motivation losses: Free-rider effects. *Journal of Personality and Social Psychology, 44,* 78–94.

Kerr, N. L., & MacCoun, R. J. (1985) Role expectations in social dilemmas: Sex roles and task motivation in groups. *Journal of Personality and Social Psychology, 49,* 1547–1556.

Kerr, R. A. (1991) Geothermal tragedy of the commons. *Science, 253,* 134–135.

Kim, O., & Walker, M. (1984) The free rider problem: Experimental evidence. *Public Choice, 43,* 3–24.

Knight, G. P., & Chao, C. C. (1990) Gender differences in the cooperative, competitive, and individualistic social values of children. *Motivation and Emotion, 13,* 125–141.

Knight, G. P., & Dubro, A. F. (1984) Cooperative, competitive, and individualistic social values: An individualized regression and clustering approach. *Journal of Personality and Social Psychology, 46,* 98–105.

Knight, G. P., Dubro, A. F., & Chao, C. C. (1985) Information processing and the development of cooperative, competitive, and individualistic social values. *Developmental Psychology, 21,* 37–45.

Knight, G. P., & Kagan, S. (1977) Development of prosocial and competitive behaviors in Anglo-American and Mexican-American children. *Child Development, 48,* 1385–1394.

Knight, G. P., & Kagan, S. (1981) Apparent sex differences in cooperation-competition: A function of individualism. *Developmental Psychology, 17,* 783–790.

Knight, G. P., Kagan, S., & Buriel, R. (1981) Confounding effects of individualism in children's cooperation-competition social motive measures. *Motivation and Emotion, 5,* 167–178.

Knox, R. E., & Douglas, R. L. (1971) Trivial incentives, marginal comprehension, and dubious generalizations from prisoner's dilemma studies. *Journal of Personality and Social Psychology, 20,* 160–165.

Komorita, S. S. (1976) A model of the n-person dilemma-type game. *Journal of Experimental Social Psychology, 12,* 357–373.

Komorita, S. S., & Esser, J. K. (1975) Frequency of reciprocated concessions in bargaining. *Journal of Personality and Social Psychology, 32,* 699–705.

Komorita, S. S., Hilty, J. A., & Parks, C. D. (1991) Reciprocity and cooperation in social dilemmas. *Journal of Conflict Resolution, 35,* 494–518.

Komorita, S. S., Parks, C. D., & Hulbert, L. G. (1992) Reciprocity and the induction of cooperation in social dilemmas. *Journal of Personality and Social Psychology, 62,* 607–617.

Komorita, S. S., Sweeney, J., & Kravitz, D. A. (1980) Cooperative choice in the n-person dilemma situation. *Journal of Personality and Social Psychology, 38,* 504–516.

Kotlikoff, L. J. (1987) Justifying public provision of Social Security. *Journal of Policy Analysis and Management, 6,* 674–689.

Kramer, R. M. (1989) Windows of vulnerability or cognitive illusions? Cognitive processes in the nuclear arms race. *Journal of Experimental Social Psychology, 25,* 79–100.

Kramer, R. M., & Brewer, M. B. (1984) Effects of group identity on resource use in a simulated commons dilemma. *Journal of Personality and Social Psychology, 46,* 1044–1057.

Kramer, R. M., & Brewer, M. B. (1986) Social group identity and the emergence of cooperation in resource conservation dilemmas. In H. A. M. Wilke, D. M. Messick, & C. G. Rutte (eds), *Experimental social dilemmas* (pp. 205–234). Frankfurt: Verlag Peter Lang.

Kramer, R. M., McClintock, C. G., & Messick, D. M. (1986) Social values and cooperative response to a simulated resource conservation crisis. *Journal of Personality, 54,* 576–591.

Kramer, R. M., Meyerson, D., & Davis, G. (1990) How much is enough? Psychological components of "guns versus butter" decisions in a security dilemma. *Journal of Personality & Social Psychology, 58,* 984–993.

Kuhlman, D. M., Camac, C. R., & Cunha, D. A. (1986) Individual differences in social orientation. In H. A. M. Wilke, D. M. Messick, & C. G. Rutte (eds), *Experimental social dilemmas* (pp. 151–176). Frankfurt: Verlag Peter Lang.

Kuhlman, D. M., & Marshello, A. (1975) Individual differences in game motivation as moderators of preprogrammed strategic differences in prisoner's dilemma. *Journal of Personality and Social Psychology, 32,* 922–931.

Kuhlman, D. M., & Wimberly, D. C. (1976) Expectations of choice behavior held by cooperators, competitors, and individualists across four classes of experimental games. *Journal of Personality and Social Psychology, 34,* 69–81.

Latane, B., & Darley, J. M. (1970) *The unresponsive bystander: Why doesn't he help?* New York: Appleton-Century-Crofts.

Latane, B., & Nida, S. (1981) Ten years of research on group size and helping. *Psychological Bulletin, 89,* 308–324.

Latane, B., Williams, K., & Harkins, S. (1979) Many hands make light the work: The causes and consequences of social loafing. *Journal of Personality and Social Psychology, 37,* 822–832.

Laver, M. (1981) *The politics of private desires.* New York: Penguin Books.

Lewis, D. (1969) *Convention.* Cambridge, MA: Harvard U. Press.

Lichbach, M. I. (1989) Stability in Richardson's arms races and cooperation in prisoner's dilemma arms rivalries. *American Journal of Political Science, 33,* 1016–1047.

Lichbach, M. I. (1990) When is an arms rivalry a prisoner's dilemma? Richardson's models and 2 x 2 games. *Journal of Conflict Resolution, 34,* 29–56.

Liebrand, W. B. G. (1983) A classification of social dilemma games. *Simulation and Games, 14,* 123–138.

Liebrand, W. B. G. (1984) The effects of social motives, communication and group size on behavior in an n-person multi-stage mixed-motive game. *European Journal of Social Psychology, 14,* 239–264.

Liebrand, W. B. G., Jansen, R. W. T. L., Rijken, V. M., & Suhre, C. J. M. (1986) Might over morality: Social values and the perception of other players in experimental games. *Journal of Experimental Social Psychology, 22,* 203–215.

Liebrand, W. B. G., & van Run, G. J. (1985) The effects of social motives on behavior in social dilemmas in two cultures. *Journal of Experimental Social Psychology, 21,* 86–102.

Liebrand, W. B. G., Wilke, H. A. M., Vogel, R., & Wolters, F. J. M. (1986) Value orientation and conformity. *Journal of Conflict Resolution, 30,* 77–97.

Lindskold, S. (1978) Trust development, the GRIT proposal, and the effects of conciliatory acts on conflict and cooperation. *Psychological Bulletin, 85,* 772–793.

Lombardo, M. P. (1985) Mutual restraint in tree swallows: A test of the Tit For Tat model of reciprocity. *Science, 227,* 1363–1365.

Lumsden, M. (1973) The Cyprus conflict as a prisoner's dilemma game. *Journal of Conflict Resolution, 17,* 7–31.

Madsen, M. C. (1971) Development and cross-cultural differences in the cooperative and competitive behavior of young children. *Journal of Cross-Cultural Psychology, 2,* 365–371.

Madsen, M. C., & Shapira, A. (1970) Cooperative and competitive behavior of urban Afro-American, Anglo-American, Mexican-American, and Mexican village children. *Developmental Psychology, 3,* 16–20.

Madsen, M. C., & Yi, S. (1975) Cooperation and competition of urban and rural children in the Republic of South Korea. *International Journal of Psychology, 10,* 269–274.

Maki, J. E., & McClintock, C. G. (1983) The accuracy of social value prediction: Actor and observer influences. *Journal of Personality and Social Psychology, 45,* 829–838.

Maki, J. E., Thorngate, W., & McClintock, C. G. (1979) Prediction and perception of social motives. *Journal of Personality and Social Psychology, 37,* 203–220.

Mannix, E. A., & White, S. B. (1992) The impact of distributive uncertainty on coalition formation in organizations. *Organizational Behavior and Human Decision Processes, 51,* 198–219.

Mansbridge, J. (1989) Love and duty: The new frontiers. *Behavioral and Brain Sciences, 12,* 717.

Marwell, G., & Ames, R. E. (1979) Experiments on the provision of public goods I: Resources, interest, group size, and the free-rider problem. *American Journal of Sociology, 84,* 1335–1360.

Marwell, G., & Schmitt, D. R. (1972) Cooperation in a three-person prisoner's dilemma. *Journal of Personality and Social Psychology, 31,* 376–383.

Maynard-Smith, J. (1974) The theory of games and the evolution of animal conflict. *Journal of Theoretical Biology, 47,* 209–221.

Maynard-Smith, J. (1976) Evolution and the theory of games. *American Scientist, 64,* 41–45.

Maynard-Smith, J. (1984) Game theory and the evolution of behavior. *Behavioral and Brain Sciences, 7,* 95–125.

Maynard-Smith, J., & Price, G.R. (1973) The logic of animal conflict. *Nature, 246,* 15–18.

McCallum, D. M., Harring, K., Gilmore, R., Drenan, S., Chase, J. P., Insko, C. A., & Thibaut, J. (1985) Competition and cooperation between groups and between individuals. *Journal of Experimental Social Psychology, 21,* 301–320.

McClintock, C. G. (1974) Development of social motives in Anglo-American and Mexican-American children. *Journal of Personality and Social Psychology, 29,* 348–354.

McClintock, C. G. (1977) Social motivation in settings of outcome interdependence. In D. Druckman (ed), *Negotiations: Social-psychological perspectives* (pp. 49–77). Beverly Hills, CA: Sage.

McClintock, C. G., & Keil, L. J. (1983) Social values: Their definition, their development, and their impact upon human decision making in settings of outcome interdependence. In H. H. Blumberg, A. P. Hare, V. Kent, & M. Davies (eds), *Small groups and social interaction* (vol. 2) (pp. 123–143). London: Wiley & Sons.

McClintock, C. G., & Liebrand, W. B. G. (1988) Role of interdependence structure, individual value orientation, and another's strategy in social decision making: A transformational analysis. *Journal of Personality and Social Psychology, 55,* 396–409.

McClintock, C. G., & McNeel, S. P. (1966) Reward and score feedback as determinants of cooperative and competitive game behavior. *Journal of Personality and Social Psychology, 4,* 606–613.

McClintock, C. G., Messick, D. M., Kuhlman, D. M., & Campos, F. T. (1973) Motivational bases of choice in three-choice decomposed games. *Journal of Experimental Social Psychology, 9,* 572–590.

McClintock, C. G., & Moskowitz, J. M. (1976) Children's preferences for individualistic, cooperative, and competitive outcomes. *Journal of Personality and Social Psychology, 34,* 543–555.

McClintock, C. G., Moskowitz, J. M., & McClintock, E. (1977) Variations in preferences of individualistic, competitive, and cooperative outcomes as a function of age, game class, and task in nursery school children. *Child Development, 48,* 1080–1085.

McClintock, C. G., & Nuttin, J. (1969) Development of competitive game behavior across two cultures. *Journal of Experimental Social Psychology, 5,* 203–218.

McClintock, C. G., & van Avermaet, E. (1982) Social values and rules of fairness: A theoretical perspective. In J. Grzelak & V. Derlega (eds), *Living with other people* (pp. 43–71). New York: Academic Press.

McNeel, S. P. (1973) Training cooperation in the prisoner's dilemma. *Journal of Experimental Social Psychology, 9,* 335–348.

Meehl, P. E. (1977) The selfish citizen paradox and the throw-away vote argument. *American Political Science Review, 71,* 11–30.

Messe, L. A., & Sivacek, J. M. (1979) Predictions of other's responses in a mixed-motive game: Self-justification or false consensus? *Journal of Personality and Social Psychology, 37,* 602–607.

Messick, D. M. (1973) To join or not to join: An approach to the unionization decision. *Organizational Behavior and Human Performance, 10,* 145–156.

Messick, D. M., Allison, S. T., & Samuelson, C. D. (1988) Framing and communication effects on groups members' responses to environmental and social uncertainty. In S. Maital (ed), *Applied behavioural economics* (vol. 2) (pp. 677–700). Brighton: Wheatsheaf Books.

Messick, D. M., & Brewer, M. B. (1983) Solving social dilemmas: A review. *Review of Personality and Social Psychology, 4,* 11–44.

Messick, D. M., & McClelland, C. L. (1983) Social traps and temporal traps. *Personality and Social Psychology Bulletin, 9,* 105–110.

Messick, D. M., & McClintock, C. G. (1968) Motivational basis of choice in experimental games. *Journal of Experimental Social Psychology, 4,* 1–25.

Messick, D. M., & Sentis, K. P. (1979) Fairness and preference. *Journal of Experimental Social Psychology, 15,* 418–434.

Messick, D. M., Wilke, H., Brewer, M. B., Kramer, R. M., Zemke, P. E., & Lui, L. (1983) Individual adaptations and structural change as solutions to social dilemmas. *Journal of Personality and Social Psychology, 44,* 294–309.

Milinksi, M. (1987) Tit For Tat in sticklebacks and the evolution of reciprocity. *Nature, 325,* 433–435.

Miller, A. G., & Thomas, R. (1972) Cooperation and competition among Blackfoot Indian and urban Canadian children. *Child Development, 43,* 1104–1110.

Miller, D. T., & Holmes, J. G. (1975) The role of situational restrictiveness on self-fulfilling prophecies: A theoretical and empirical extension of Kelley and Stahelski's triangle hypothesis. *Journal of Personality and Social Psychology, 31,* 661–673.

Mischel, W. (1968) *Personality and assessment.* New York: Wiley.

Murnighan, J. K. (1991) *The dynamics of bargaining games.* Englewood Cliffs, NJ: Prentice-Hall.

Murnighan, J. K., & Roth, A. E. (1983) Expecting continued play in prisoner's dilemma games: A test of several models. *Journal of Conflict Resolution, 27,* 279–300.

Musgrave, R. A. (1959) *The theory of public finance.* New York: McGraw-Hill.

Northcraft, G. B., & Wolf, G. (1984) Dollars, sense, and sunk costs: A life cycle model of resource allocation decisions. *Academy of Management Review, 9,* 225–234.

Olson, M. (1965) *The logic of collective action.* Cambridge, MA: Harvard U. Press.

Orbell, J. M., & Dawes, R. M. (1981) Social dilemmas. In G. Stephenson & J. H. Davis (eds), *Progress in applied social psychology,* vol. 1 (pp. 37–66). Chicester: Wiley.

Orbell, J. M., & Dawes, R. M. (1991) A "cognitive miser" theory of cooperators' advantage. *American Political Science Review, 85,* 515–528.

Orbell, J. M., van de Kragt, A. J. C., & Dawes, R. M. (1988) Explaining discussion-induced cooperation. *Journal of Personality and Social Psychology, 54,* 811–819.

Osgood, C. E. (1962) *An alternative to war or surrender.* Urbana: U. of Illinois Press.

Oskamp, S. (1971) Effects of programmed strategies on cooperation in the prisoner's dilemma and other mixed-motive games. *Journal of Conflict Resolution, 15,* 225–259.

Oye, K. A. (1985) Explaining cooperation under anarchy: Hypotheses and strategies. *World Politics, 38,* 1–23.

Palfrey, T. R., & Rosenthal, H. (1983) A strategic calculus of voting. *Public Choice, 41,* 7–53.

Parker, G. A. (1970) The reproductive behavior and the nature of sexual selection in *Scatophaga stercoraria* L. (Diptera: Scatophagidae) II: The fertilization rate and the spatial and temporal relationships of each sex around the site of mating and oviposition. *Journal of Animal Ecology, 39,* 205–228.

Parker, G. A. (1978) Selfish genes, evolutionary genes, and the adaptiveness of behavior. *Nature, 274,* 849–855.

Parker, G. A. (1984) Evolutionarily stable strategies. In J. R. Krebs & N. B. Davies (eds), *Behavioural ecology* (2nd ed) (pp. 30–61). Oxford: Blackwell Scientific Publications.

Parker, R., Lui, L., Messick, C., Messick, D. M., Brewer, M. B., Kramer, R., Samuelson, C., & Wilke, H. (1983) A computer laboratory for studying resource dilemmas. *Behavioral Science, 28,* 298–304.

Patchen, M. (1987) Strategies for eliciting cooperation from an adversary. *Journal of Conflict Resolution, 31,* 164–185.

Pettigrew, T. F. (1978) Three issues in ethnicity: Boundaries, deprivations, and perceptions. In J. M. Yinger & S. J. Cutler (eds), *Major social issues* (pp. 25–49). New York: Free Press.

Pilisuk, M. (1984) Experimenting with the arms race. *Journal of Conflict Resolution, 28,* 296–315.

Pilisuk, M., Potter, P., Rapoport, An., & Winter, J. A. (1965) War hawks and peace doves: Alternative resolutions of experimental conflicts. *Journal of Conflict Resolution, 9,* 491–508.

Pilisuk, M., & Rapoport, An. (1964) Stepwise disarmament and sudden destruction in a two-person game: A research tool. *Journal of Conflict Resolution, 8,* 36–49.

Pilisuk, M., & Skolnick, P. (1968) Inducing trust: A test of the Osgood proposal. *Journal of Personality and Social Psychology, 8,* 121–133.

Pilisuk, M., Winter, J. A., Chapman, R., & Haas, N. (1967) Honesty, deceit, and timing in the display of intentions. *Behavioral Science, 12,* 203–215.

Platt, J. (1973) Social traps. *American Psychologist, 28,* 641–651.

Plous, S. (1985) Perceptual illusions and military realities: The nuclear arms race. *Journal of Conflict Resolution, 29,* 363–389.

Plous, S. (1987) Perceptual illusions and military realities: Results from a computer-generated Perceptual Dilemma. *Journal of Conflict Resolution, 31,* 5–33.

Plous, S. (1988) Disarmament, arms control, and peace in the nuclear age: Political objectives and relevant research. *Journal of Social Issues, 44,* 133–154.

Poppe, M., & Utens, L. (1986) Effects of greed and fear of being gypped in a social dilemma situation with changing pool size. *Journal of Economic Psychology, 7*, 61–73.

Pruitt, D. G. (1983) Experimental gaming and the goal/expectation hypothesis. In H. H. Blumberg, A. P. Hare, V. Kent, & M. Davies (eds), *Small groups and social interaction* (vol. 2) (pp. 107–121). London: Wiley & Sons.

Pruitt, D. G., & Kimmel, M. (1977) Twenty years of experimental gaming: Critique, synthesis, and suggestions for the future. *Annual Review of Psychology, 28*, 363–392.

Ptashne, M., Johnson, A. D., & Pabo, C. O. (1982) A genetic switch in a bacteria virus. *Scientific American, 247*, 128–140.

Radner, R., Myerson, R., & Maskin, E. (1986) An example of a repeated partnership game with discounting and with uniformly inefficient equilibria. *Review of Economic Studies, 53*, 59–69.

Rapoport, Am. (1985) Provision of public goods and the MCS experimental paradigm. *American Political Science Review, 79*, 148–155.

Rapoport, Am. (1987) Research paradigms and expected utility models for the provision of step-level public goods. *Psychological Review, 94*, 74–83.

Rapoport, Am. (1988) Provision of step-level public goods: Effects of inequality in resources. *Journal of Personality and Social Psychology, 54*, 432–440.

Rapoport, Am., & Bornstein, G. (1987) Intergroup competition for the provision of binary public goods. *Psychological Review, 94*, 291–299.

Rapoport, Am., & Bornstein, G. (1989) Solving public good problems in competition between equal and unequal size groups. *Journal of Conflict Resolution, 33*, 460–479.

Rapoport, Am., Bornstein, G., & Erev, I. (1989) Intergroup competition for public goods: Effects of unequal resources and relative group size. *Journal of Personality and Social Psychology, 56*, 748–756.

Rapoport, Am., & Eshed-Levy, D. (1989) Provision of step-level public goods: Effects of greed and fear of being gypped. *Organizational Behavior and Human Decision Processes, 44*, 325–344.

Rapoport, An. (1960) *Fights, games, and debates.* Ann Arbor, MI: U. of Michigan Press.

Rapoport, An. (1964) *Strategy and conscience.* New York: Harper & Row.

Rapoport, An. (1967) A note on the index of cooperation for prisoner's dilemma. *Journal of Conflict Resolution, 11*, 101–103.

Rapoport, An., & Chammah, A. M. (1965) *Prisoner's dilemma.* Ann Arbor, MI: U. of Michigan Press.

Riker, W. H., & Ordeshook, P. C. (1968) A theory of the calculus of voting. *American Political Science Review, 62*, 25–42.

Roth, A. E. (1991) Game theory as a part of empirical economics. *Economics Journal, 101*, 107–114.

Rubenstein, A. (1989) The electronic-mail game: Strategic behavior under "almost common knowledge." *American Economic Review, 79*, 385–391.

Rubin, J. Z., & Brown, B. R. (1975) *The social psychology of bargaining and negotiation.* New York: Academic Press.

Rutte, C. G., & Wilke, H. A. M. (1985) Preference for decision structures in a social dilemma situation. *European Journal of Social Psychology, 15*, 367–370.

Rutte, C. G., Wilke, H. A. M., & Messick, D. M. (1987) Scarcity or abundance caused by people or the environment as determinants of behavior in the resource dilemma. *Journal of Experimental Social Psychology, 23*, 208–216.

Sampson, E. E., & Kardush, M. (1965) Age, sex, class, and race differences in response to a two-person non-zero-sum game. *Journal of Conflict Resolution, 9*, 212–220.

Samuelson, C. D. (1991) Perceived task difficulty, causal attributions, and preferences for structural change in resource dilemmas. *Personality and Social Psychology Bulletin, 17*, 181–187.

Samuelson, C. D., & Messick, D. M. (1986a) Alternative structural solutions to resource dilemmas. *Organizational Behavior and Human Decision Processes, 37*, 139–155.

Samuelson, C. D., & Messick, D. M. (1986b) Inequities in access to and use of shared resources in social dilemmas. *Journal of Personality and Social Psychology, 51*, 960–967.

Samuelson, C. D., Messick, D. M., Rutte, C. G., & Wilke, H. (1984) Individual and structural solutions to resource dilemmas in two cultures. *Journal of Personality and Social Psychology, 47*, 94–104.

Samuelson, P. A. (1954) The pure theory of public expenditure. *Review of Economics and Statistics, 36*, 386–389.

Sandler, T., & Murdoch, J. C. (1990) Nash-Courant or Lindahl behavior? An empirical test for the NATO allies. *Quarterly Journal of Economics, 105*, 875–894.

Sattler, D. N., & Kerr, N. L. (1991) Might versus morality explained: Motivational and cognitive bases for social motives. *Journal of Personality & Social Psychology, 60*, 756–765.

Sawyer, J. (1966) The altruism scale: A measure of cooperative, individualistic, and competitive interpersonal orientation. *American Journal of Sociology, 71*, 407–416.

Schelling, T. C. (1960) *The strategy of conflict.* Cambridge, MA: Harvard U. Press.

Schelling, T. C. (1973) Hockey helmets, concealed weapons, and daylight saving: Binary choices with externalities. *Journal of Conflict Resolution, 17*, 381–428.

Schelling, T. C. (1978) *Micromotives and macrobehavior.* New York: W. W. Norton.

Schelling, T. C. (1984) *Choice and consequence.* Cambridge, MA: Harvard U. Press.

Schlenker, B. R., & Goldman, H. J. (1978) Cooperators and competitors in conflict. *Journal of Conflict Resolution, 22*, 393–410.

Schroeder, D. A., Jensen, T. D., Reed, A. J., Sullivan, D. K., & Schwab, M. (1983) The actions of others as determinants of behavior in social trap situations. *Journal of Experimental Social Psychology, 19*, 522–539.

Schulz, U. (1986) The influence of social orientation and generalized expectancies on decision making in iterated experimental games. In R. Tietz, W. Albers, & R. Selten (eds), *Bounded rational behavior in experimental games and markets* (pp. 95–110). Berlin: Springer-Verlag.

Sen, A. (1977) Rational fools: A critique of the behavioral foundations of economic theory. *Philosophy and Public Affairs, 6*, 317–344.

Shaw, J. I. (1976) Response-contingent payoffs and cooperative behavior in the prisoner's dilemma. *Journal of Personality and Social Psychology, 34*, 1024–1033.

Shepperd, J. A., & Wright, R. A. (1989) Individual contributions to a collective effort: An incentive analysis. *Personality and Social Psychology Bulletin, 15*, 141–149.

Shippee, G. (1980) Energy consumption and conservation psychology: A review and conceptual analysis. *Environmental Management, 4*, 297–314.

Shubik, M. (1968) On the study of disarmament and escalation. *Journal of Conflict Resolution, 12*, 83–101.

Shubik, M. (1970) Game theory, behavior, and the paradox of the prisoner's dilemma: Three solutions. *Journal of Conflict Resolution, 14*, 181–193.

Simon, H. A. (1957) *Models of man.* New York: Wiley.

Simon, H. A. (1990) A mechanism for social selection and successful altruism. *Science, 250*, 1665–1668.

Skinner, B. F. (1953) *Science and human behavior.* New York: Macmillan.

Smith, V. L. (1979) An experimental comparison of three public good decision mechanisms. *Scandinavian Journal of Economics, 81*, 198–215.

Smith, V. L. (1980) Experiments with a decentralized mechanism for public good decisions. *American Economics Review, 70*, 584–599.

Smolensky, E., Becker, S., & Molotch, H. (1968) The prisoner's dilemma and ghetto expansion. *Land Economics, 44*, 419–430.

Snidal, D. (1985a) Coordination versus prisoners' dilemmas: Implications for international cooperation and regimes. *American Political Science Review, 79*, 923–942.

Snidal, D. (1985b) The game *theory* of international politics. *World Politics, 37*, 25–57.

Snyder, G. H. (1971) "Prisoner's dilemma" and "chicken" models in international politics. *International Studies Quarterly, 15*, 66–103.

Snyder, G. H, & Diesing, P. (1977) *Conflict among nations.* Princeton, NJ: Princeton U. Press.

Spicer, M. W. (1985) A public choice approach to motivating people in bureaucratic organizations. *Academy of Management Review, 10*, 518–526.

Staw, B. M. (1981) The escalation of commitment to a course of action. *Academy of Management Review, 6*, 577–587.

Steele, M. W., & Tedeschi, J. T. (1967) Matrix indices and strategy choices in mixed-motive games. *Journal of Conflict Resolution, 11*, 198–205.

Stern, P. C. (1976) Effect of incentives and education on resource conservation decisions in a simulated commons dilemma. *Journal of Personality and Social Psychology, 34*, 1285–1292.

Stern, P. C., & Gardner, G. T. (1981) Psychological research and energy policy. *American Psychologist, 36*, 329–342.

Stingle, S. F., & Cook, C. (1985) Age and sex differences in the cooperative and noncooperative behavior of pairs of American children. *Journal of Psychology, 119*, 335–345.

Stroebe, W., & Frey, B. S. (1982) Self-interest and collective action: The economics and psychology of public goods. *British Journal of Social Psychology, 21*, 121–137.

Suleiman, R., & Rapoport, Am. (1992) Provision of step-level public goods with continuous contribution. *Journal of Behavioral Decision Making, 5*, 133–153.

Swap, W. C., & Rubin, J. Z. (1983) Measurement of interpersonal orientation. *Journal of Personality and Social Psychology, 44*, 208–219.

Tajfel, H., Billig, M., Bundy, R., & Flament, C. (1971) Social categorization and intergroup behavior. *European Journal of Social Psychology, 1*, 149–178.

Taylor, M. (1987) *The possibility of cooperation.* Cambridge: Cambridge U. Press.

Tedeschi, J. T., Hiester, D., & Gahagan, J. P. (1969) Matrix values and the behavior of children in the prisoner's dilemma game. *Child Development, 40*, 517–527.

Teger, A. I. (1980) *Too much invested to quit.* New York: Pergamon Press.

Terhune, K. W. (1968) Motives, situation, and interpersonal conflict within the prisoner's dilemma. *Journal of Personality and Social Psychology, Monograph Supplement, 8*, 1–24.

Tetlock, P. E., McGuire, C. B., & Mitchell, G. (1991) Psychological perspectives on nuclear deterrence. *Annual Review of Psychology, 40*, 239–276.

Thibaut, J. W., & Kelley, H. H. (1959) *The social psychology of groups.* New York: Wiley.

Toda, M., Shinotsuka, H., McClintock, C. G., & Stech, F. (1978) Development of competitive behavior as a function of culture, age, and social comparison. *Journal of Personality and Social Psychology, 36*, 835–839.

Trivers, R. L. (1971) The evolution of reciprocal altruism. *Quarterly Review of Biology, 46*, 35–57.

Turner, J. (1978) Social categorization and intergroup differentiation in the minimal group paradigm. In H. Tajfel (ed), *Differentiation between social groups* (pp. 101–140). New York: Academic Press.

Turner, J. C., Brown, R. J., & Tajfel, H. (1979) Social comparison and group interest in ingroup favoritism. *European Journal of Social Psychology, 9*, 187–204.

Unger, R. K. (1979) *Male and female: Psychological perspectives.* New York: Harper & Row.

van de Kragt, A. J. C., Dawes, R. M., Orbell, J. M., Braver, S. R., & Wilson, L. A. (1986) Doing well and doing good as ways of resolving social dilemmas. In H. A. M. Wilke, D. M. Messick, & C. G. Rutte (eds), *Experimental social dilemmas* (pp. 177–204). Frankfurt: Verlag Peter Lang.

van de Kragt, A. J. C., Orbell, J. M., & Dawes, R. M. (1983) The minimal contributing set as a solution to public goods problems. *American Political Science Review, 77,* 112–122.

van Lange, P. A. M., & Liebrand, W. B. G. (1991a) Social value orientation and intelligence: A test of the Goal Prescribes Rationality Principle. *European Journal of Social Psychology, 21,* 273–292.

van Lange, P. A. M., & Liebrand, W. B. G. (1991b) The influence of other's morality and own social value orientation on cooperation in the Netherlands and the USA. *International Journal of Psychology, 26,* 429–447.

van Lange, P. A. M., Liebrand, W. B. G., & Kuhlman, D. M. (1990) Causal attributions of choice behavior in three n-person prisoner's dilemmas. *Journal of Experimental Social Psychology, 26,* 34–48.

von Neumann, J., & Morgenstern, O. (1947) *Theory of games and economic behavior.* Princeton, NJ: Princeton U. Press.

Wagner, R. H. (1983) The theory of games and the problem of international cooperation. *American Political Science Review, 77,* 330–346.

White, R. K. (1977) Misperceptions in the Arab-Israeli conflict. *Journal of Social Issues, 33,* 190–221.

Wilke, H. A. M., & Braspenning, J. (1989) Reciprocity: Choice shift in a social trap. *European Journal of Social Psychology, 19,* 317–320.

Williams, K., Harkins, S., & Latane, B. (1981) Identifiability as a deterrent to social loafing: Two cheering experiments. *Journal of Personality and Social Psychology, 40,* 303–311.

Wilson, W. (1973) Reciprocation and other techniques for inducing cooperation in the prisoner's dilemma. *Journal of Conflict Resolution, 15,* 167–196.

Wrightsman, L. S. (1966) Personality and attitudinal correlates of trusting and trustworthy behaviors in a two-person game. *Journal of Personality and Social Psychology, 4,* 328–332.

Wrightsman, L. S. (1991) *Assumptions about human nature.* Newbury Park, CA: Sage.

Wrightsman, L. S., O'Connor, J., & Baker, N. J. (eds) (1972) *Cooperation and competition.* Belmont, CA: Brooks-Cole.

Wyer, R. S. (1969) Prediction of behavior in two-person games. *Journal of Personality and Social Psychology, 13,* 222–228.

Wyer, R. S. (1971) The effects of outcome matrix and partner's behavior in two-person games. *Journal of Experimental Social Psychology, 7,* 190–210.

Yamagishi, T. (1986a) The provision of a sanctioning system as a public good. *Journal of Personality and Social Psychology, 51,* 110–116.

Yamagishi, T. (1986b) The structural goal/expectation theory of cooperation in social dilemmas. *Advances In Group Processes, 3,* 51–87.

Yamagishi, T. (1988a) Exit from the group as an individualistic solution to the free rider problem in the United States and Japan. *Journal of Experimental Social Psychology, 24,* 530–542.

Yamagishi, T. (1988b) Seriousness of social dilemmas and the provision of a sanctioning system. *Social Psychology Quarterly, 51,* 32–42.

Yamagishi, T. (1988c) The provision of a sanctioning system in the United States and Japan. *Social Psychology Quarterly, 51,* 265–271.

Yamagishi, T., & Sato, K. (1986) Motivational bases of the public goods problem. *Journal of Personality and Social Psychology, 50,* 67–73.

Zimbardo, P. G. (1970) The human choice: Individuation, reason and order vs. deindividuation, impulse, and chaos. *Nebraska Symposium on Motivation, 17,* 237–307.

INDEX

and experience, 96–97
and family economics, 141–42
and free-choice versus leaders, 92
and individual solutions for, 91,
    95–100
and partitionment, 94–95
and punishment, 99–100
and social identity, 97–99
solutions for, 91–100
structural solutions for, 91–92
Resources, 61
Responsibility, and diffusion of
    responsibility, 46
Reward, 11, 17, 22–25, 41, 128
Rijken, V. M., 90, 115
Riker, W. H., 54
Rocke, D. M., 127, 133
Rogers, A. C., 86
Rosen, B., 69
Rosenthal, H., 137
Roth, A. E., 38–39, 153
Rubenstein, A., 133
Rubin, J. Z., 85, 109
Rutte, C. G., 88–90, 93, 94, 154

Saint, 28
Sampson, E. E., 121
Samuelson, C., 82
Samuelson, C. D., 88–89, 90–91, 92,
    93–94, 96, 154–55
Samuelson, P. A., 54
Sanctioning system, 74–75
Sanctions, and free ride, 74–75
Sandefur, C. A., 86
Sandler, T., 141
Sato, K., 49, 73–74, 108
Sattler, D. N., 115
Sawyer, J., 105, 107
Schaerfl, L. M., 95
Schelling, T. C., 7–8, 14, 44–45,
    125–26, 131, 133
Schlenker, B. R., 33, 114
Schmitt, D. R., 45–46
Schroeder, D. A., 90
Schulz, U., 114
Schwab, M., 90
Second-order dilemma, 48–49
Security dilemma, 128–31
Self-efficacy, 55–62
Seller, and buyer, 138–41
Sen, A., 149

Sentis, K. P., 94
Sequence dilemma, 113, 114
Sex, and social values, 121–23
Shaklee, H., 29, 69, 114
Shapira, A., 119, 121, 122
Shaw, J. I., 31–32
Shepperd, J. A., 64
Shinotsuka, H., 119
Shippee, G., 154
Shortcut, 94
Shubik, M., 127
Similarity of preferences, 132
Simmons, R. T., 71
Simon, H. A., 130, 148
Sinner, 28
Sivacek, J. M., 114
Siverson, R. M., 127
Skinner, B. F., 11
Skolnick, P., 126–27
Slovic, P., 94
Smith, V. L., 76–77, 125
Smolensky, E., 141
Snidal, D., 127, 131, 132
Snyder, G. H., 127, 128
Social dilemmas
    and discrepant findings, 155–56
    and energy conservation, 154–55
    examples of, 152–55
    and fishing in Atlantic Ocean, 152
    and future research on, 155–56
    general definition, 8–13
    and incentive programs, 153–54
    and interdisciplinary issues. See
        Interdisciplinary issues
    introduction to, 1–15
    and political science, 125–38
    and public goods. See Public goods
    and steam power, 152–53
    summary and conclusions, 151–56
    and symmetry, 133
Social exchange, 3, 14
Social fence, 11, 85
Social identity, 97–99
Sociality, as rationality, 149–50
Social loafing, 64
Social traps, 8, 9–10, 11, 14, 80–100
    behavior in, 86–91
    and communication, 95–96
    and conformity, 88–90
    defined, 81–86
    and experience, 96–97